M000307043

Sincerity
is the new happy

© 2018 Kristen B. Shaw

All rights reserved. This book or any portion thereof may not be reproduced or used in any manner whatsoever without the express written permission of the publisher except for the use of brief quotations in a book review.

ISBN 978-0-9975670-6-9

Published by Bluebullseye Press

Book design © John H. Matthews
www.BookConnectors.com

Cover design by Megan Bradley

Sincerity
is the new happy

kristen b. shaw

bluebullseye press

for my family & friends. Joseph Campbell for

seeing the magic that exists, The Secret for

positive thinking, Deepak Chopra for the mirror,

The Dalai Lama for kindness, Tony Robbins for

action, Buddha for letting go, Eckhart Tolle for

now, and mother Theresa for love.

Contents

Introduction   1

Section 1 ~ happy ego
Chapter 1   5

Section 2 ~ thrashing ego
Chapter 2   33

Section 3 ~ destructive ego
Chapter 3   47
Chapter 4   55

Section 4 ~ letting e go
Chapter 5   71
Chapter 6   87
Chapter 7   105
Chapter 8   117
Chapter 9   125
Chapter 10   131

Introduction

I'd like to make a toast to "***sincerity now being the new happy***" today, starting with me!

Sincerity is key in attracting positive energy and true love, right? Sincerity is when our heart, words and actions are all in harmony, right? Sincerity is a great life strategy if thoughts are creating our reality, right? I still complain of what isn't, even though the universe has delivered the best it knows how. I have always lived in a nice home and still have two legs and two arms that I am grateful for. I am currently married to a dish of a finance guy and mother to a bumbling Viking of a ten-year-old who kicks the ego out of me all day long! This is the story of how my jet-fueled, unstoppable, ego could have taken away my genuine happiness, appreciation for other people and sincerity (which is very dear to me).

Being humbled by working in France where the people speak a German blend (breathe), by progressive trance house boat parties on California's Great Lakes (breathe), while sobbing, sweating and climbing eleven mile Hawaiian cliffs -- just for play (breathe), to continually getting rehired (breathe) from my racing mind (pause), made me consider (pause) (pause) that other people's realities, stories and ways to happiness were more interesting than mine.

Share with me, if you would please, a large glass of this sincerity w a splash of happy. Let's blend our thoughts, words and actions into delightful responsibility, happy detachment and sunshine, starting right now. First sip is the best, I promise!

Section 1

happy ego

Chapter 1

"childhood & young ego is an adventure like no other. Each day brings you closer to who you will become."

- kkshaw47

upside of ego

"does ego create hope? I think so."

- kkshaw47

Ego makes our dreams come true, right? There is a huge upside. The ego created the planet. I have been riding my ego for years and bedazzled by others egos and success my entire life. I love others egos, they are fascinating to observe. Ego created love, education, art, architecture, poetry, painting, building, exploring, dancing, business, farming, aeronautics, lacrosse, football, basketball, education, amusement parks, writing, the internet, advertising media, books, pop songs, moguls, motivational speakers, humans to look up to, hope. Does ego create hope? I think so.

my ego's useful ways in family's chaos

There really is not one perfect person on the planet, so how can there be a perfect family? My parents took very nice care of my sister, brother and me. We were as normal a family (for the 70's) as any. What does that mean exactly? The best of times were spent with my parents, Tom and Jane, and my two siblings, Abby, four years older than I, and TJ (now Tom), three years older. My parents had an iron-tight relationship and friendship. They were equally well read in world politics, colorful with their kindness and fiery temperaments, as they sipped and saluted their way through life riding my Dad's F-14 career at rocket speed!

The universe blessed me with a working family and good health despite the cigarette smoking while I was still in my mother's womb (this is the 70's, Mad Men style, right?). It also gave me a determination to live big moments, and thrive in the world. My feisty ego drove me through my parents' chaos to find the most exciting and hip centered school friends in the world, according to me.

I am happy for that chaos because that was where I was. My family living was fun, dynamic and dismal. Aren't all families? My friendships were a sanctuary for sincerity, no judgment and never-ending, sun blazing, bikini beach days. In childhood and in my young adulthood, the universe was in the <u>queue</u> to give me—everything!

Jane and Tom rocked many patio gatherings under the stars, through the hot blistery nights along Long Island's South Shore back in the 70s. In winter, happy & festive dinnertime was in the bright green and orange plaid kitchen.

"Parents just got to relax & party."

I get it now.

Both of my parents grew up in Long Island, NY. My mom, Jane, a very attractive, blue-eyed girl from Argyle Park in Babylon Village, voted Most Cheerful in her graduating class, met my dry-witted, arrogant (see the ego starting here?) dark-skinned, dark-eyed Irish father, Tom, on the Long Island Railroad in 1951.

My father's grandparents had come from Brooklyn by way of Galway, and during my father's childhood years, summered in South Hampton. Tom Kane Jr., my father, was distinguished, tan-skinned with black slightly wavy hair and light brown eyes. He was adorable & sarcastic with quirky one liners. He was a "balls to the wall" Navy- fighter- pilot guy who wore super bright, electric green, narrow, whale, corduroy, pants while continually smoking cigarettes. My father was a self educated (prior to his receiving an MIT Sloan School of Business degree in 1971), well-traveled individual. His motto was "fuck off" to anyone or anything that he could see through. He had a bored and condescending candor with me as a child, which became sugar coated as I grew older. We had little in common when I was a teenager. However, as I traveled more, we found our way to one another. Through our exploring of (his far and away more than mine) people and places, we met each other, whether with captains of Hawaiian luxury vessels by the Aloha Tower, the Maître d's at The Jockey Club in Arlington, VA or at the Babylon Village firehouse beer blast.

My parents were handsome and not without their raging egos. They were sophisticated for the 70s because they looked down on racism and tried their best not to be judgmental of others. They tried! It isn't easy in the suburbs.

They were not child-centric. They tried, but it did not come naturally. They were very good providers who enjoyed taking us to the beach and loved dinner hour. That was where we bonded over a green salad, a steak, Italian bread and an amber bottle of Cold Duck that we later made into a drip rainbow candle.

It was so dear for my parents to have family dinner. I am happy I belonged to someone, somewhere. I am so thankful for my parents' strength as members of our community. They had each other's back, their smoking, drinking and laughter into the late nights. They stood behind everything that they said and did. I have to admire them for that. My family gave me iron strong bonds to everything that they stood for – respecting other people, rejecting racism, discussing Republican and Democratic politics at length while watching the evening news.

In 1972 my father became a Marketing VP at Grumman Aerospace. He was a highflying salesman of his time for bringing in mega defense contracts home to Grumman headquarters in Bethpage. He traveled to Iran in 1971 and brought home a huge F-14 Tom Cat order (3 billion dollar deal) that next summer.

Tom was home at 7 pm on weekdays and left before we woke up so he could read The New York Times before daily briefings in his office. When at home, he was reading quietly and smoking cigarettes. Jane, my mother stayed at home with my brother, sister, our dachshund, and me just like the 70's show. I'm telling you! She has a strong willed character and she learned early on that you have to nurture yourself when you're a mother, so when the children leave, you are not left with your vague self. She pursued her bridge game, solid girl friendships, and artistry of water coloring that she enjoys to this day.

I have to hand it to her. It was always about her. I so get it now. She preferred her own space to anyone else. She has got some rocks, my mother Jane. My parents were much stronger and smarter than I am. They were a united front of authority in our family, and it helped me see their "message."

They were on one side of the equation and we (my sister, brother and I) were on the other. Their strong bond, was good for them, but not always good for us.

My mothers' parents, Ed and Julie McGinnis also lived in Babylon Village. We spent time with them while my father was traveling for business. This was important, because someone else was disciplining us, and we needed it. My grandmother Julia Hamm, from Toulon, Illinois, came to New York, went to Bayshore's Nursing School and became the head maternity nurse at South Side Hospital in the 1930's. My grandfather Ed McGinnis, with cherry red cheeks like Santa Claus, came from Clinton, New York and was a civil engineer who assisted in constructing highways up and down Long Island. He also played his fiddle for the Prohibitionists out on eastern Long Island during the years. My grandfather was "a present adult." He was happy to talk, listen and appreciate children. Grandpa was such a dear! He was a father figure to my older brother Tom. He took him hunting with their chubby beagle girl, Teddy, and golfing at the Brightwaters Country Club. My father Tom Kane Jr., traveled 100 days out of the year, he was a work road warrior! What excitement it was (for him, not sure about us) to sell F14's to the world at that time. I'm not too sure now though.

It was perfectly normal for my grandparents Ed and Julie to be merrily enjoying their golf outing lunches that lasted for several hours. I am shaking my head right now, because they did function well. Again this was the 1970's. I cannot think of one night of my life, where my parents Tom and Jane and my grandparents Ed and Julie were not celebrating life under the stars from the humid hot summers into the blistery cold winter. Happy New Year!

My father's father, Tom Kane, and my grandmother, Jean Kane, were great grand children of Kelly green immigrants from Ireland, by way of Brooklyn. When my grandparents got married in the year 1931 and had three children, my grandfather was 21 years old. Soon after, he went to Shanghai, China and sought to buy a feather manufacturing import/export business.

Who goes on the road at that age with a family and brings home an empire?

As a result the family was well-off Irish on Long Island. My grandfather developed Kane & Company on 8 Wall Street in New York. I never met my grandfather. My grandmother Jean Kane was strong and pleasant (from what I remember as a very young child) who lived close by in Bay Shore. My grandfather passed away from kidney failure and the family business deteriorated because of bad managing and ego behavior. My father told me he left Manhattan College, to work at Kane & Co after his father died. There was great disrespect going on between my uncles who were in charge at that time. He then left to pursue his career in the Navy. My father had a comfortable childhood enough, though not without difficulty.

My parents had fabulous fun at dinner hour, either in the kitchen during the cold winter nights or laughing under the backyard stars in the summer. They could push the limits of fun because the next day there was little energy for us. Don't get me wrong; I had a childhood ball in the rambunctious neighborhood on Copper Tree Lane. We spent summer family vacations on Fire Island and many hot August days at the Babylon Yacht Club terrorizing anyone in our path, as kids do. We very often tried to find our way, through the "shut down" during cocktail hour – ask any kid who grew up in the 70's. As a child, I wished my parents were like other parents, (ate dinner at 5pm, went to the amusement parks and the movies as a family, lol) but it eventually taught me an acceptance of family's inevitable chaos.

God bless them all for their parenting mantra. It was we do what we want and there are no excuses, ever. Knowing now what I know as a mother it makes all the sense in the world! It just isn't that great when you are the children trying to navigate your parents to the end of dinner. Let's go home now please!

Right, everybody?

All goes well when well is well.

I call my family egotistical and reactive crazy because everybody's anger was more important than mine! I had to let go of my parents dysfunction, which was ignoring me, telling me I spoke too much, and that I really could never do anything all that interesting, which may have been true. They never consciously put me down, 'cause I was dear enough. It's just the way it was. It meant go find your own confidence through experience, right?

I truly had an ideal childhood because I can see now it was not perfect. If it had been perfect I might have been in more trouble. Cocktail hour is pretty and fun when it starts out, with the hot yellow summer flowered or snowman napkins, with little plates of hors d'oeuvres that are heavenly because of their size when you are little. However, sometimes, not always, the happiness and laughter could become angry, sloppy and mean after the sun set.

My mother was my father's rock and she forgave him no matter how hammered he could be after his evening tastings.

With my family's inevitable chaos, I needed to find a way to wrangle myself out of the dim feelings I had from my parents' self-importance. A result was my sister, Abby's overly emotional behavior from my parents' minimal neglect each day and my brother's detachment and wondering (like me), what happens when the sun finally sets. I had a burning desire to go elsewhere and feel less invisible.

We were friendly with this wonderful Irish family from The Crescent Street in Babylon. Their father Dr. Tommy McLoughlin was a pediatric surgeon and their mother was Mary Eileen, a very dear old friend of my mother's from Babylon village. They had four children. Our parents would have their cheery spirited dinner parties and howl and laugh into the late night. In third grade, we rented a house on Harbor Island in the Bahamas for a week during Spring break. We headed out from NY to Florida and then took a small military plane (I had my sand pail and bucket) to Nassau. From there, I will never forget this small boat of a Mako, with all of our luggage, James Bond style, thrashing in the pale green sea with our knee socks and navy boat sneakers and boys in their pin striped ties. You had to dress up on airplanes back then. I remember at the airport on the way down there, all parents went into the bar for Virgin Bloody Marys, and left us seven children outside to wait for them. I think we were anxious that we would miss our plane, but we made it.

We rented a pink and white shabby chic kind of house with waving palm trees and exotic shrubs all around the gardens, right in the heart of town. It was so interesting for the time it was. This plantation house had two hard working, tired, but smiling cooks Ruth, who made the most delicious lemon fried chicken and Debbie, who had a one -year old baby name Urslie. I could not stop looking at his beautiful baby self. We ran all over that island with the local children on their mini bikes and inhaled Slurpee's and Cadbury chocolate bars from Piggly Wiggly all day long. Parents cannot possibly keep a close eye on all of their children. I was the third child and on my own to have fun, all within reason. It was a gift for sure. I could have used some bedtime reading and guidance perhaps, but being left alone taught me how to see the world through my eyes. My dear neighbor, Playboy pin up with German cheekbones and Carly Simon hips, Irene Morris said once, "Kristen, you must have sat in your playpen by yourself for 4-5 hours one sunny day when you were around 1 year old."

I think maybe that is why I love the birds chirping so much. I was happy enough, so who cares? I was on my own to sit, play, go out and do what I wanted, within reason. It was very helpful for me to have an imagination and run off and find anyone who would play with me. My childhood best friend, was Denise Verderosa, an only child, four-years-old when her moving truck pulled into Kingsland Place around the corner.

Denise's mother Enes Verderosa told me recently, "You were standing outside of this truck, at five years old, with dirty bare feet, messy pigtails, at probably 9 in the morning."

We were best friends for 10+ years and it was the most fun of my life. "Only" children get to swim on fancy swimming teams. They go to child playhouse theaters, they go to ice skating rings and generally are entertained a lot of the time. My house was fun because we were under the radar, which is cool too.

The best part of the starry night patio parties was early the next day. After my mother's prickly attitude had vanished by sleeping, would wake up with her angelic, adorable voice, feeling new and happy. My father wore his distinguished suit again, my sister's golden brown eyes smiled, and my darling brother Tom and I, who understood the chaos the same way, in acceptance, were always ready for the new day!

My family's deeply rooted ego gave us the best of times with friends, the beach and travel, while giving me a tough turtle shell, that got me through snowboarding the cliffs of extreme adventure and letting go of feeling invisible again.

letting go w/ attention deficit disorder

I have textbook ADD, even though I have not been formally diagnosed. I have always had it and I always will.

ADD is brutal in school and once you learn that its part of you, you better get organized early in the day just to barely keep up with everyone else. I believe that my father had a bit of ADD, but he coped with it well and he went into sales and that was a great place for him and me too, later on. I was a fantastic reader in second grade, very social, but as I got older, I could not retain information easily at all. I would take notes and not remember 98%. I would study at length and score average on my tests. I was very up and very down. Having ADD humbled me in school. Every day I wanted to perform well, but I had roller coaster grades. Every student wants to be a classroom star and do well in class. Every student wants to have good listening skills and perform in studying and testing. Why can't the education system see this? Either I did 100% of what was being asked of me on an exam or there was a blank page where I could not comprehend anything after reviewing the science or reading material for hours.

My ex-husband once said, "You start your stories and conversations in mid-sentence, but there is no beginning or end." It is such a perfect analogy. I can become uninterested very easily, which is brutal for my loved ones, particularly Brady: "Mommy, why do you always walk out of the room?" Is there any point to starting anything if you can't finish? My poor husband is like, "Oh, my god, girl." "I'm like, sorry, lamb."

In school, I just did not comprehend what most teachers said, only a handful of ones that were patient. I have difficulty following directions correctly --if at all. In 8th grade I was tested for possible learning disorders. The guidance counselor reviewed the information with me; I completely forgot everything and became angry and then tearfully sad. It was textbook ADD right there, thank you very much. My diagnosis of ADD was written right on the wall, but they determined that I was an emotional person and that is why I could not remember. Interesting right? I do not believe that they knew what this was exactly. But that is life too – you know. One of the attributes of ADD is that you learn to let go of what everybody else is scoring and doing, because you cannot think like them at all. Your grades will show your lack of focus, time and time again. Studying is memorization and I do not have that skill. You got the wrong lady for that.

While being humbled by my family's inevitable chaos, where the egos ruled the roost, being humiliated by my frenemy, ADD, I had a bright spirit, and was ready to roar and banter with girlfriend classmates, interested in me.

my ego's social ways

"The privilege of a lifetime is being who you are."
                                        - Joseph Campbell

We grew up Catholic and I am thankful to the church for allowing me to be a princess for my First Holy Communion. My family really tried to feel the love and guidance. I never felt the love, of course. I was trying my hardest not to be bored out of my mind (because ADD makes you crazy bored and you just can't help it). Always the sermons are to be better and not selfish, but I still did not see their loving kindness behind their smiles. They seemed inauthentic to me.

Mr. Lobasso's twelfth grade in 1980 Comparative Religion class gave me a glimpse of hope. His introduction to Islam, Hinduism, Confucius, and Taoism made religion compelling, bright and interesting. I had Mr. Lobasso in tenth and eleventh grade for history. These history classes were a grind and required a lot of writing and reading and listening. He made you listen and think. He grilled me and compartmentalized me as miss party girl who thought my words were more interesting than anyone else's - sigh.

I proved to be a different student in Religion class. Mr. Lobasso dismissed me less because I could not keep my attention from his words on Confucianism and the power of Tao. The section on Islam went for three months at the very time that the fundamentalist Islamists were beginning to target the West. I was determined to do well in this one class that seemed to come easy somehow.

Joseph Campbell is the spiritualist of a lifetime! He lived as an American professor, writer and lecturer on comparative mythology and religion. His work covers many aspects of the human experience. The fact that Campbell, a Sarah Lawrence scholar, was discussing religion in a free spirited and poetic way was a relief for me. His message in folk tales, architecture, and eastern wisdom emphasizes the role of the "hero." A hero is someone who has given his or her life to something bigger than his or her self. He literally spoke with stars in his eyes. He mentions that eternity has nothing to do with time. He describes the pain and suffering of the world as part of the mosaic art form of the universe. He confirms, "This is the eternity and this is the heaven and bliss we should be living and nothing more."

I had to let go of my parents' chaos in the best way that I could. I was a little bird looking for a place to perch and drink some water. I found peace, love and understanding with my girlfriends from 1969 until now! As my family was occupied at all times with work and socializing, I found my girlfriends in Babylon Elementary & Grade school one year at a time.

As a young girl from a nice family I was a bully on the school bus. Kids from the bus will tell you. I believe it was peer pressure or physical energy I was burning and just felt it rushing through my limbs. I would harass girls for no reason and had a fistfight with a boy on my bus in third grade. I would get punched, get up, fix my dress, and shake it off. See how my ego was working for me then? I really had been pushed and hit by my mother's best friend's son and once I stood up for myself, at the age of seven, I felt invincible. It was necessary! Childhood & the young ego is an adventure like no other. Each day brings you closer to who you will become.

friends are like flowers

"I have a wonderful garden of golden yellow daffodils, blushing pink tulips and a rainbow of late summer zinnias that I call my friends!"

–kkshaw47

As I got older I found that my sincere friendships were a sanctuary. I could be myself, more than with my family. I believe this is true for all of us, right? My squad, the IBTC (itty bitty titty committee) were all girls from Babylon, New York, born in 1963, that understood how to have fun within reason, to be trustworthy (and not bullshit insincere) and thirsty enough for the hearty adventure!

I remember in 1977 when Fleetwood Mac's *Rumors* came out. We could not play that record enough. It was the summer and we smoked massive amounts of Salem Lights at Field 2 Fire Island. Led Zeppelin & Pink Floyd penetrated the blurry heat wave during the hot days of summer in 1977, 1978, and 1979. Mind you, we could rock an Indian Batik bikini like no other at 13, 14 and 15 years old. We were flower children of acceptance from early on (we did not attach negatively to anything or anyone, ever), before the egotistical husbands showed up and the demands of parenthood. We had all the ingredients for blending fun, puffing and sipping good vibrations in the sun with loving kindness that saved my soul.

Let's toast a magnificent cheer to having the most fun (within reason) Sex in the City of Babylon style, of anyone on the block! Green Apple Hookah tastes anyone? I tasted other very colorful things in the early 80s. I sampled East Coast orange sunshine mixed with white cap powder flakes from South America during those years. Glad I made it back from the rainbow!

My friendships were the rocks of adventure and adoration. I grew up with friends who were sincere and became key trustworthy relationships in my life. These were friendships that developed from kindergarten, to second grade, to fifth grade, to sixth grade, and to seventh grade.

In kindergarten, I met on the playground seesaw, Laurie Saccacio at four years old wearing a sailor's suit dress with white bow, can you imagine how beautiful she was? She rode the hot Harleys in San Francisco with me and now is back in Babylon going to her "meetings" to keep her on the bright path. In second grade class, I met, Jackie Navarro, now an early childhood educator with the wisdom of God's light at a young age. She wrote happy poetry that the boys took time to listen to. In fifth grade, I met brilliant future Cornell graduate Susan Campisi. She is Italian with beautiful dark spiraled hair. She has perfect Material Girl complexion and physique like Madonna. She has spent most of her life along the West Coast drinking Americanos from Seattle's strongest coffee shops to drinking Harper Moons in sunny, free, and breezy Pasadena, California. She now rescues pit bulls and battles corrupt ivory factories in China from Los Angeles, which is a badass job, everyone. By the way – Susan's guidance and patience in my lifetime has been a treasure. She suggested early on that I start writing and helped me upload my first blog. She's truly the best, always willing to listen. Never putting her self first. In middle school, I met Nordic looking Cindy Sparks (sparkles for eyes, let me tell you) who will literally give you her heart and conquer the imbalances of this earth with her voice. My Virgo Denise Penney went up in United's friendly skies of aeronautical schooling in Daytona Beach and has been an airline pilot for 30+ years. Seventh grade I met Claire Bear. She is an Irish beauty with silky brown hair (and a voice like an angel) that could firmly manage any project at Coopers Lybrand, and be trusted with a secret till the end of time. Lastly and always is Sarah Kain. Sarah is a childhood friend with golden sunflower colored eyes, streaming blond hair whose been designing clothing made out of imaginative recycled fabric for years.

My mother, Jane, used to say, "Tell me who your friends are and I will tell you who you are." I have a wonderful garden of daffodils, tulips and colorful zinnias that I call my friends!

Our intention (my friends and me) was to rocket into this world and drink as much fun and excitement as possible. Sip of ego, anyone? There was only room to grow with the universe and no judgments at all. Otherwise there is no point. We were dancing to life's rhythms that taught us how to respect one another and seek to take this world's wild ride as safely as possible.

Throughout those years these friendships provided water, sun and nourishment to one another that made me who I am today. I trust, adore, cherish, and wish people well. I attribute this to my friendships. When you have ADD you want to alter your mind because, when it is spinning you cannot focus. We were sampling purple micro dots going back-to-school in 1978, to enjoying spirited happy hours at 7 AM in 1979 while successfully making the gymnastics team. We were getting our "happy on" every step of the way.

We made our fun happen, while living in sincerity 100%. We were going to study as hard as possible, after our football, gymnastics and field hockey - just try and not blaze too much before tryouts!

Did anyone see the IFC channel film, *Dazed and Confused* (in the best way possible)?

This was the foundation of my personality, and it was so helpful for me to be as a person. I will always and forever be grateful to my friends growing up in Babylon Village. My friends loved me no matter how much (still do) energy I sucked out of the room. If there was jealousy it was not spoken of. Did we lose our self-importance for the sake of our circle of friends? We were sexy too-- let me tell you. We did not hold back on laughter, adventure, or making out with the cutest guys we could find. Were they the cutest? They were to us!

We were honest, truthful, high spirited and not interested with what anyone said or thought, we did not even notice because we were on our own heavy ego trip. We wore our first grade bell bottoms together, seventh grade Indian boutique shirts with pucca beads, first tans listening to Peter Frampton "Comes Alive" on Fire Island in 1976 and going to the The Lynyrd Skynyrd concert in 1979: "Hold this. I can't stop coughing." We had our first puffs and Pabst Blue Ribbon black outs; we did everything in a unified matter. We were the IBTC (the Committee they would call us) and we were super good at it. Country style 70's partying elevated into 80's Miami Vice of snow shoveling style right into the decade of 90's Nirvana grunge flare in San Francisco.

We loved one another unconditionally. Right you guys? Did I get this right? These friendships nurtured individualism, trust, and were positive in every way. Growing up in Babylon gave me very close friendships that shaped my ongoing values and the key relationships. These friends taught me how to be good, bad, and me. They served as my family unit for many years; they were always there to pick me up from my dim averages in school, the continual job terminations, my allergy to happy hour and later, my not-without-drama-divorce.

My friends were there for me during my raging ego years. Some pumped my ego like a balloon and others watched in stillness waiting for me to pop and get over myself already. "Lights out" because it is last call of your raging ego crush of a cocktail, one too many! I am grateful beyond words for my friendships. This is why I do not understand insincerity, which is bad karma.

> *"You can talk shit about your family, but not best friends because they are all we have to trust in this world".*
>   – kkshaw47

We have always trusted one another with shit talking. I honestly did not say anything unfavorably about any of my dear & pretty girl friends that I would not say right to them. Talking shit about others can potentially manifest bad karma, according to Mr. Deepak Chopra.

"Deepak Chopra is an American author, public speaker, alternative medicine advocate, and a prominent figure in the New Age movement. Chopra gained a following in 1993 after his interview on the *The Oprah Winfrey Show* regarding his books.[9] He then left the TM movement to become the executive director of Sharp HealthCare's Center for Mind-Body Medicine and in 1996 he co-founded the Chopra Center for Wellbeing." – Wikipedia. He helped me understand the downward spiral of self importance and that we are a mirror reflection of ourselves. It was and still is profound.

My friends were sincere and awesome and there was no bullshit ego. There was nothing "wrong" to say. Perhaps that is why bullying is so medieval & infantile in its nature. Who can you trust in this world if you don't have solid relationships to nurture you along the path of life? You can talk shit about your family, but not your best friends because they are all we have to trust in this world. Where are the friends in your life to keep your shit together when you are stumbling? I was grateful for my friendships then & now. These were my friends that would say, "Girl, you were so loud last night. You inhaled too many Thin Lizzy's! Next time can you shut the fuck up? We still love you, though."

Forgiveness in friendship is the greatest asset. It keeps everything humming along, even if previous circumstances are not ideal. My friendly lambs could tell me their house was burning down; they had no money, and they stayed up all night while devouring the snow on their boyfriend's mirror. I learned a level of trust and sincerity with myself and others during those years that keep me grounded today.

I had more bitch slap sessions with my sister when I was a kid than with any of my friends. My friends were the rocks that kept me from hating myself or shit talking too much at other people's expense or being negative in general. They spent time with me when my family was acting out their own detachment. I think so many of us go to our friendships for the comfort that our families did not give us. Our mothers were overwhelmed (with our older brothers and sisters) and our fathers did not give a shit about anyone, but themselves.

Does this sound familiar? My friendships brought me poetry, spirituality, love, grace, help, trust, strength as my own family does now. My friends have always been in the pursuit of decent husbands, bouncing babies, and great adventures. And the thought of light and grace has always been a key point in our conversations.

No shit talking please, I need good karma today!

When the universe delivers great friends like I had, how could I nourish this garden to keep me going? With friendly love, respect and no judgment, right? From childhood to now it was and is, poems of love, smoking spirits bright, Jackie's poetry for spiritual protection, births of our children, singing silly love songs, traveling, sampling x, writing more poetry, getting divorced, moving to Europe, snorting Colombian train rails—all with friends shaking and gliding around the globe for days, months and years. These unique pals gave me the idea to speak French as they went on student archeological digs in countryside France, other friends studied kabuki in Japan, they got me cocktail waitressing on Hawaiian cruise ships, and some of them moved to California with me.

The sunset orange zinnias, blush pink peonies, and popping yellows daffodils in my garden, I call my friends, is a bouquet like no other.

failure

> "*Three things that cannot be hidden: the sun, the moon and the truth.*"
>
> – Buddha

Failure is a truth to my story. I am proud of my mistakes because they are mine.

From third grade on, it was difficult to concentrate, so let's get this over with. Grade school was joyous because I met so many kids and found the best girl friendships out there. School was a double-edged sword for me. I had successful friendships in grade school and they carried me to senior year. My ADD, which took over the short-term memory part of my brain, often left me in emotional shambles. I went to three different colleges to earn a basic liberal arts degree. I got an A plus in socializing and sampling flower power juice, but my academic grades were not stellar, even though I studied. I was not a person that did not care about my grades.

The two saving graces for me at the time were my mother and father, also social creatures who did not perform ideally in school. They wanted to do well too! Therefore they were never looking for the top grades, just passing so you could get a job. I am thankful for the pressure they did not put on me, because then I would be more spastic than I already was or am.

My friends (many of whom are very successful in academics and careers) were there when my ADD failed me and in my thriving career (not). They never compared me to anyone but - me!

For me it is a special gift. It gave me the persistence to have to work extra hard with ADD. An ADD mind is racing so fast it has difficulty actively listening and there is no short-term memory. In my life I have to try very hard to stay in check and listen. I am 100% Dory from Finding Nemo. Nice enough, but alarmingly forgetful at times? I have a hard time telling a story in depth because I forget. My mind is a pinball machine and I have to love it because it is mine. I am 54 years old and I do not understand the most basic things. Anything over two thoughts and I'm outta here!

Poor everyone that loves me. In my school years, after the school day, I would go to special learning groups, get tested by our fifth grade level teaching neighbor Irene Morris, and they would say, this is emotional. I was not diagnosed, thank goodness. Because it taught me how to live in the way my mind is wired, without Ritalin or Adderall because that is a whole other neurotransmitter story. The only way to embrace my disorder is to say, I do not think like everybody else no matter what I do or try! I do not have the cognitive ability, never have and never will. I have big time cognitive challenges! I could study for hours and try and understand the concepts of exams, but at the end of the day the information is gone the very next day or even the same moment. ADD broke my heart in school. I do not believe there is any child that does not want a great grade average. The kids with ADD can't study because they don't know how or there is not the right environment for it. We zone or crumble when a boring person begins to speak, it's our truth and it is infuriating for someone to speak to us. Perhaps schools should have classes to teach super high energy racing minded ADD students with lots of ability to start ambitious projects, formative ideas or assemble A Team committees – and have them work with students who demonstrate valuable implementation skills. Success!

I always try hard to focus and comprehend at any job and I love working so much! It keeps my brain moving along. I can start anything. If you want me to develop a concept or business idea for you – I am awesome at that. But you have to manage it after that because I will forget what I started, seriously.

The positive take away with ADD is that we like to work and keep working hard.

My friends would lift me up every time I failed a critical final or college entry test (after studying beforehand) or was "let go" from a job—I needed to survive!

"my friends never compared me to anyone but me!"
– kkshaw47

I do not know how people do not get fired. I always do. At the end of the day no matter what I did, talked to management about what I could be doing better or did not say enough, I was let go. I do not speak corporate America or higher education, no matter what.

Some friends can be kind to your failures, and others cannot. My friends were NYC stockbrokers, early childhood development teachers and airline pilots, parents, or in graduate school and I was running around the Bay Area as a temp receptionist. My friends were there for my issues, even when my family could not have cared less. My friends were accomplished.

And I tried, you know? Accepting myself for that has been a relief. If I keep going and working and taking full responsibility for it all, then my expectations are real and the outcome is real and I can only learn from working harder. My sales manager at Penguin Computer, Howard Johnson (in the depths of San Francisco Tenderloin with Tommy the Vietnamese server seller and Patrick the proud Chinese gentlemen from The East Bay) wrote on my sales pipeline update email, "Never surrender and never give up!" My menu of jobs when I arrived in San Francisco included typing a book for David Sheff of Beautiful Boy, selling life insurance as a broker, grape seed oil demonstrator of Napa Valley gourmet products and Hula Sisters Swimwear sales lady to name just a few! See how I am starting many projects with all of this zest?

I loved that I got my ass kicked from my multiple failures because then I would not have learned what hard work; persistence and gratitude (happy today) can do for you. I would be the biggest asshole if the universe gave me everything I ever wanted too soon in life. My ego would have ruined my sincerity, destroyed my love and faith for everybody and everything! I am experienced enough to know that one-day your life is here and the next day it can change and you have to get over yourself, the best cocktail ever!

I went to a junior college in Franklin, Massachusetts with my very best friend from Babylon, Jackie Navarro, whose poetry and understanding of "light" provided a delightful journey of fun and adventure and still does.

sip of me? anyone?

I learned about non-stop traveling back then. My sophomore year was very fun, and I had the dearest friends from Connecticut and New Jersey. The Grateful Dead was on any time they were in the dorm. Dear Sarah and Laura Brady, you nice kind ladies from Summit, New Jersey, were the best. They were impeccable Dead Heads too, sophisticated partiers acting like grownups, making their own money to get to the shows and making their grades even if it meant staying up all night taking "mini thins" to study. At Dean Junior College I scored an internship my sophomore year during the Christmas break at Good Samaritan Hospital Islip in the dietitians' department. They were so nice to me and I did so little. Simple filing. Anyway, I made enough money to fly myself to Los Angeles and visit my newlywed sister and brother-in-law. I remember my camel-colored leather pants getting me bumped up to first class and drinking Sauvignon Blanc the entire flight and laughing with a Richard Dreyfus giggly kind of guy. I was trashed by the time I got there. My grades were decent at Dean Junior College and I moved on to and was accepted into American University in Washington, DC in 1983.

This was exciting for my parents since Tom, my father, boarded the Gulf Stream each week to the Grumman DC office. I was in the international dorm on the floor with the other transfer students. I was living and gossiping with Rania from Israel, Lena from Beirut,

Lena from Kuwait, and another Lena from Lebanon! There was the slithery 80's lanky girl Alex from The Main Line, her bubbly Connecticut roommate Stephanie, and lastly a very punk-looking girl from Patterson New Jersey, Maria Rabat, a Syrian American. She was an adorable, smart, pixy- punk of a girl who knew her Russian literature, hands down.

Finally, during the first week of American University as a transfer student, I met a spunky, absolutely darling, peppermint Patty of a girl from Perth Australia, Kerstin Norlin. She came bumbling into the community room, with pep and spunk, big green eyes and big boobs, according to the guys. We became fast friends and tore through the halls of AU. We drank and smoked until the cows came home while ice-skating Columbian mirrors with the purest intentions. It was at AU in DC that I learned about the world. I discovered what a provincial, talkative (and not in a good way) fat ass of a bumpkin I was. Yikes. It was a huge growth spurt.

Nothing can prepare you for a cosmopolitan existence when you've spent comfortable days in the wonder bread suburbs. By second year, first semester, I was in deep academic trouble and my parents were paying a lot of money for this bachelor's degree. The classes were large and I could not retain anything and I was so uncomfortable in my own skin. I have a heavy heart thinking of this. I returned to AU on probation, where I met the queen bee of it all, Christina Thurmer from Boulder Colorado in Political Science.

Christina was a very tall girl wearing ballet slippers and an Iranian pashmina, with a perfectly crooked smile. She is stunning because she is so cool. She gave me my coolness, I swear. At that time, she wore a real leather purse; freesia perfume called Antonio's Flowers and organic lip-gloss. She drove a convertible white Rabbit. She was friendly with the fancy-speaking Iranians. She never studied and she made the best grades. Her major was Public Relations, which to this day I do not understand as a profession, but that is normal for me.

She has and will always have the biggest ego of anyone I know, which is entertaining, to say the least. She is from the family of the founders of the American Express Empire by way of New Canaan to Boulder. I love her so much and she is another friend who taught me how to live. We were always eating - hotdogs, cheese, pickles, ratatouille, and nachos- nothing specific, just everything. But we both can rock a bikini to this day for some reason (at 54 years old our days are numbered, for sure). Christina is in continual search of the groovy people. Christina's friends are "the" life style people, who are the musicians & artists of Marin county, #8 Facebook employees, Pixar creators, and the northern California activists who produce the structures at Reno Nevada's Burning Man, to name a few.

I remember being friendly with her from the beginning. The night I met Christina she'd just returned from a two-week stay in Negril Jamaica on $1 per day. This seemed to be a very hip and cool place that I would never see because I never had enough money or guts to move and travel around like that. Christina's ADD is epic like mine. We were on the party path in DC also, St Elmo's Fire style. No, really!

One day in Georgetown, in front of our favorite bar, Third Edition, there was a camera crew and sound booms, directed at Rob Lowe in costume as Billy with the layered hair and earring. I had never even seen him before except once in a magazine. It so happens that they were acting in the movie St. Elmo's Fire, which is what we were living each day, drinking, shoveling snow during the summer, taking the Metro to Capitol Hill and being with a group of best friends. That time was an awakening to the world for me. Washington, DC is an international city with every language and person on the planet.

I couldn't study once I moved in to Christina's town house in Georgetown! If I tried to read a chapter in school, she would start talking, put snow flurries in my coffee cup and turn up the Roxy Music. Cheers to my failures! My parents somehow understood my failing grades, my happy hours, my lack of focus, my continual socializing, doesn't matter, they know I tried! I remember the day at the Jockey Club in DC, my handsome father putting sugar in his clean ice tea and shaking his head and saying, "Well it's time to go to New York." You are being fired from college! For many years, failure was a truth for me. Its just the way it was, the more I reached, the more I failed.

Section 2

thrashing ego

Chapter 2

I went home that summer to multiple interviews and landed my first job on 57th & 5th at Dreyfus as the admin to the Creative Advertising Department. One year after that, I received a call to interview for president admin of international start up company that provided administrative services.

I got a job in 1986 in New York working for Mark Lamela, President of Intergest USA. This was a small, global company that provided administrative services with consulting, logistical, distribution services, etc. for any company that wanted to have business in another country. I could not type a letter without an error and my "white out application" was worse. I like perfection and no matter what I do, I cannot keep it together with administrative work. I try to! It escapes me. I was responsible for filing and keeping it all together. This was the beginning of my melting down.

During this employment, I had the opportunity to work for Intergest France (these people had blinders on to my limited French speaking ability).

failure

"I needed to get lost to find myself. I did too!" – kkshaw47

One of my obsessive visions was to live in Europe (like my friends from BV). I moved to northeastern France, to a small industrial, most un-Aix-en-Provence place in the country. I had a job as an administrative assistant with a pool of 21 French secretaries.

There was little hazing from these ladies, considering I was moving from the big NYC to a smaller office in Alsace Lorraine. They presumed I was a high-powered, French-speaking number cruncher who could burn through deals with the big CEO. Oh, boy! The pool of secretaries managed 100% administration (banking, correspondence, taxes, etc.) from HQ in the petite village of Sarreguemines, France. These women were effective business people in a small rural village. In the beginning, my colleagues and I revealed that my French was dire and I was never going to get an "administrative contract" from a German cabinetry company, ever. My French Americana was weak and everybody's English improved at that time (sigh).

By the end of my internship in France, I was fetching cafe and l'etoile pastries and candy bons bons! I became the girl Friday! I did everything I was supposed to with a smile and determination (and, trust me, I had no idea what I was doing). That is where my nickname KK started. My new name grew like a vine in France and applies to this day.

French people are icy at first, but when they love, they will love you forever. They adored my New York chaos. This is where I first became unglued. Living abroad, away from the east coast, getting up for work, driving to the office to push through wall after wall of uncertainty, was my first drop kick into the abyss. The crispy Alsatian wine helped that along too! It was a grand time and one of the hardest hurdles of low self-confidence in my ability to overcome.

During these years I was anxious about what I did not understand. I could not speak French (after being in Europe for six months) and it was degrading to me. Everyone thought I was a stupid American too, because they all spoke a colorful variety of languages like German, French, and Italian to start with.

I am insecure and this was just the beginning of it all. I needed to get lost in order to find myself. I did too! This rapid growth spurt #2 (DC was #1) was forcing me to grow and learn that life is vast everywhere and fitting in culturally takes time. I had to go to the ruby red & gold colorful garden of zinnia's, my friends, to discuss the "crazy within" during that time in France. I was writing letters and I was lost in a sea of super rural French people and all I did was work. It was an unusual experience. The summer before I returned to NY from this European stay, I traveled to Greece with my French roommate. One July evening in 1988, off the Islands of Athens we sat around a blazing bon fire with wholesome young people from France, Greece, Italy, Sweden and Denmark, like in the film *The Beach* but without trance house music – that would come later in California. This Greek island adventure kept me alive & well (still confused) and moving like a dolphin. Once I returned to France from Greece, I left for Italy solo (in 24 hours). I made my way to the beach side communities of Northern Italy called the Cinque Terre. This beach community was one homemade margarita pizza after the next with sunshine and refreshing Pino Grigio. I met Solveig and Ingeberke from Trondheim, Norway. These sweethearts from Scandanavia kissed and romped every adorable lamb in Monteresso (Scandanvian people are so honest & true). They were delightful! One night I remember riding with a buff, well groomed friend of the Italian guy, (not the guy of course) and two of us on his Vespa, warm air above and the stars. We were just letting our hair flow up and down the perfectly cobblestoned streets.

Just before my lady friends were about to cruise up north back to Trondheim, we decided to have a picnic at the Leaning Tower of Pisa. We were happily drinking Chianti and eating cheese. I said, "I am coming with you to Norway".

We boarded a euro rail in Milan and chugged to Hamburg. The Hamburg train swam to Copenhagen (the San Francisco of Scandinavia) and up to Sweden and, boom, right to Trondheim, Norway, which felt like California.

God bless my parents for believing in my wanderlust and paying my entire credit card while there. WTF KK! They were furious with me, as they should have been. I was going to follow my bliss no matter what. Mr. Joseph Campbell is smiling (from heaven) at me right now. I stayed in the girls' Nordic hometowns and found the culture to be unique and as progressive as it gets. One family I stayed with, at length, were super liberal elitist Apple programmers. We went hiking in the fjords and ate heart shaped waffles with Gouda chesse sliced on top, every day.

So after working in France, traveling to Greece, Italy & Scandanavia that summer, I returned to New York. The office was silent. Mark, my boss had demoted me for not wanting to kiss his old bones (on a short trip to Europe while I was there), who would? Back at the office in New York and in France, I tried not to take anything for granted and be thankful for this, but I felt terrible, helpless and like a puddle about having to quit, because administrative work is not my calling.

After my experience in France I felt that nothing could challenge me more than listening, comprehending and then barely speaking another language. I ended my days at Intergest USA (boss was cheering) and got ready for some warm weather.

I started to shake the drink of worldly happy mix. Here I come world --cheers, santé, and down it!

ego's continual path to happy adventure

My Ali Larder-looking friend Dianne Jeurgens Kinnear was a fancy pastry chef at Le Bernadin in NYC in the later 80s. In 1989 she got a job aboard the Monterey Princess vessel from Norway that took excursions throughout the Hawaiian Islands. I pleaded with her to get me out of NY and onto the ship with her. I would do anything to leave NY. In March that year, I boarded this huge ship and began a weekly circulation of splashing to the Islands of Kauai, Maui, and The Big Island and back to Honolulu. Aboard the ship, Dianne introduced me to the hung over laundry girls from Seattle WA, rich kids from Missouri, the big tanned sweet Trixie waiter dude, a blonde god with a heart of gold. I was hired as a cocktail waitress running the decks of the ship with my rough brown loafers and smoking herb with this frenzied, funny, Portuguese Hawaiian, then 35-year-old, girl named Maili from Kaui!

Just before our ship sailed, Dianne and I went to the Ilikai Hotel and leveled the most sushi that I can remember. From there we took our tipsy selves to The Wave where we met a guy named Ohm, a Brown University student taking a semester off to teach scuba diving. We began an outward-bound happy trails excursion every moment we were not working on the cruise ship. We went from one lit up campsite to the next.

We did the most camping in Kauai. We ate our Easter dinner in a tent. We went into a candlelit Sufi dance in a cave singing healing vibes to a young man unable to walk. The ceremony leader was a kind, older woman with a crown of flowers. She was dragging around homeless teens and so loving towards them.

I felt great magic and warmth that night in the cave while preparing to head on a 13-mile hike to Kailua Valley trail. Nature was big for me on this hike. Once I hiked the thirteen miles, the amateur in me was beat up with unbearably painful blisters, dehydrated, constipated and bitchy tired. However, when we arrived there was a two-mile wide beach waiting for us. It was Shangri La. We met two LA actors inside this sanctuary at the beach and went to the waterfalls. There were more trees than you could imagine. At one point after sitting in the pond for a couple of hours, I felt intimidated by a dragonfly, of all things. This was how small I had become in the ruling tower of nature. I could not hold a candle to this pillar of Mother Earth's power.

My hiking partner, Ohm, was experienced. He was educated on the importance of yoga, breathing and deep meditation are to survive on this planet. He was a determined Buddhist back in 1989. I am thankful to him for introducing me to the concept of Buddhism and the happiness it can bring!

I felt like I could go and be anywhere without any fear after France and now Kalalau Valley. At this point, I was feeling ready for my own walk on Mars. What more could the universe provide me?

So much more, I thought (sigh).

I arrived at SFO June 2 1991. Christina was waiting in her off-the-shoulder cotton white shirt, cool washed denim jeans and white mommy Keds. She was a frenzied mother of a one year old, I get it now! A tall Nick-Cage-then looking guy accompanied her to the airport that day. He was the guy I went to see the stars with at the Golden Gate Bridge, the last time I was in San Francisco.

Christina Pettigrew is a tall drink of refreshing fun, curiosity and good living. I had never seen organic, pesticide-additive-preservative-free on everything. She was shopping in Whole Foods and eating organic goods since forever. I mean this was Marin County!

Her husband Jim Pettigrew, a tree man at the time and observer of nature at its best, had the great Mike Collins (an organic farmer friend of theirs) from Healdsburg, CA come and literally rip up their entire lawn on Shell Avenue to rid it of any pesticide soil. I remember on a cold spring morning, Christina was looking out at her desert of a backyard, and thinking is this the right thing to do? It was.

The Nick Cage looking guy at the airport with Christina, and I became good enough romantic partners for five years before we got married in 1995. He showed me all the fun ways to live in San Francisco. The thrift-shopping on Haight Street, eating Greek dinners with German biker friends and picnic beach days at Half Moon Bay, Pacifica and Sunset Beach!

The German New Year's Eve tradition is to go to the garage, give everybody an instrument and begin to play. Just keep playing. After 11 minutes (which is a long time in band minutes) you start to get some kind of rhythm going and it is as uplifting as the afternoon clouds under a blue sky in Wyoming. On Sunday afternoons, we'd go to The Zeitgeist, and I would watch people drink! There I was with my Irish knit cable sweater in a sea of black-leathered SF street bikers riding Harley Davidsons.

Nick Cage, the boyfriend at the time, blew up his quota and we attended the 1992 Oracle sales conference in Maui. The ultimate memory is Larry Ellison, a Zuckerberg elite type back then, sitting motionless in a raging party of relational database reps. That was life then. I was convinced the world owed me everything, by the way. Didn't it?

I did not have job experience when I came to SF. The Bay Area is a sophisticated city. It is where the Internet was born! Bay Area residents are competitive, educated, or they are the 1%. My SF friends were running profitable businesses, had trust funds, or were leaping (not climbing) up the corporate ladder at Gap Inc. or in Silicon Valley. They were badass.

I was obsessed with copywriting. I went on multiple interviews that year. I could not get an internship to write for advertising. I should have kept at it. I took a writing class with a Green Advertising copy writing exec and it felt like a calling. We were creating tag lines for strawberry farm campaigns and other awesomely colorful ideas like Tax CEOs (in 1991). I was good at it. I could not get a copywriting job in advertising to save my fucking life. It just did not work out. I forgot about this dream, 'cause I had to pay the SF bills.

i am always working

Thank you to all of my loved ones who see how I spin all day long. Short-term memory loss is ADD, right? We look insane because we are distracted and putting order to the chaos that we just forgot about. ADD is exhausting for loved ones and friends to observe.

I could not get a job for one solid year. I had to support my $1000 a month living expenses while having a different job every week. I could be exaggerating, but I probably had 12 jobs before The Gap hired me! I kept getting temp jobs because there were no jobs in SF during 1991-1993. I worked in architectural firms, a printing company, the Aids Dance-A-Thon with Queen Latifah, she was awesome! I worked for a charter sailing company in Sausalito and also edited the book *Atari* for David Schepp who wrote Beautiful Boy. I babysat for the beautiful boy in Sausalito. He was beautiful.

After almost a full year of hard-core job-hunting, I got a call back to be the assistant to Nancy Watkinson, Director of Store Communications at Gap, Inc. She was my first boss and understood me for the grunge pop tart I was. She gave me the patience and tools to get projects done, be successful, and she praised my work! I will be thankful to her forever.

marriage #1 , the abyss

By now I had been in a relationship with this Nick Cage looking guy for several years. Perhaps we should have called it off at 3 months, you know? With this husband, everything was an emotional chore. It seemed like the more I convinced others how great this relationship was, the more it was slipping away. I was talking and not listening, mostly to myself. Through those years of failures and escapades my ego began to over serve me, by my feeling inadequate. I mean this is how it goes. Thankfully my nights then were not drink-filled, but fun-filled for sure. We were beginning to go our separate ways while in a marriage. There were no more happy picnics at the beach, no more bike trips to Lake Tahoe or scrabble games at Farleys. It was a brutal silent tug of ego and war. The saddest days ever!

We blame our partners for our failed relationships. But we sign up for it with bells on. Marriage is a choice in the United States of America. This type of husband I had was an intelligent and good person. He is also a 100% multi-dimensional manipulator, meaning he has lots of conversations in his head to benefit himself. Sorry, dude, but you are the king of manipulation. Good luck with that karma!

We sought counseling and like many of these cases, the psychologist asks the wandering partner practically under oath, and they will say, with a twitch, I do not love another, but they do! After eleven sessions of marriage counseling where he withheld everything about his feelings towards me, he confessed that he did not want to be with me.

Here comes the road not taken.

I began a career in sales that to this day I am grateful for. Never thought I would do that.

Sales is the perfect job for people with ADD (because it allows you to thrive on self-starting and actualizing work that you manage mostly yourself) and the reward is worth it even if it is scary (ADD makes you hyper and unable to sit still. Food additives, processed sugar maybe?). I was lucky to have good managers who would supplement my administrative shortcomings. Each morning at 6 AM, with my heart on my sleeve, I would drive down 101 to Palo Alto (Facebook headquarters) and cold call pitch government agency IT departments , selling ad hoc query tools that allowed users to sort out data on reports by departments (sales and finance) of your business. I loved speaking to people and setting up appointments for my reps who were out in the field. I could not do enough for my reps and they appreciated me. They were not frowning upon my mistake ridden administrative performance. I learned how to be self-generating and resourceful. You may see sprinkles of my salesmanship while I tell this story. Someone has got to keep pushing, right?

In addition to my ADD, I had to ride the Jedi of sales excitement through the late 90s and early 2000's that turned out to be sometimes hard, more times fun. I did have a unique way of prospecting and pitching my sales calls. It was the best and then it stopped abruptly as the tech bubble started to burst.

My account management job at XUMA was a high tech roller coaster ride and not without everyday anxiety. This company was the best social experience. See me with the social edge again like in grade school? The CTO, Jamie Lerner, motor crossing, west coast cowboy, turned ice man for a minute, had the best parties. All of sales and tech engineers would take x at his house, not me of course! We had a tech conference on the Lake Shasta houseboats. The beating, hissing and hip house trance took over our entire sales department. Sales people are always up for the "random." I continued working sales jobs in network admin, hosting, and a construction company that developed clean rooms in Silicon Valley. Finally, after the state insurance test. I became an insurance broker for Select Quote. I loved that job, sales pit and my manager. Just when all was well at SelectQuote, I moved home to New York to business develop at the New York Sun Newspaper in Tribeca. The Sun was a great sales pit but, another nail-biter with the quotas! I had my last job in NYC at Yahoo Hot Jobs, which I look back on fondly. My manager Seth Weingarten was the greatest kid, he was like 18 years younger than me and I made him stress so many times from promising to close a 50K deal that I found over the phone.

Through all these follies, I was getting hired, blaming others because of my failures and talking to make up for my inadequacy. When things are going my way, I am the most agreeable and loving person. However, if I sense insincerity (which is betrayal in a way), I become a defensive and reactive person. We should have a health class in high school on how to detach from negativity. We talk about positivity which is easy, how do we detach from negativity to keep living in happiness? We all have or will experience betrayal. Its part of life, right? On this planet earth, negativity is inevitable. This is where we all go wrong, even the most honored great men and women can be corrupted by reactive, defensive and egotistical behavior.

My gnarly ego ale was refreshing & delicious even when it brought out the negative side of me; I was thirsty! Still!

Section 3

destructive ego

Chapter 3

When I was left to fend for myself; I scrambled, tumbled, clawed, rose up and fell back down again. The road not taken, revealed the negativity in me.

I alienated myself from my best friends, because they didn't do what I wanted. See the ego lurking at all times? Don't get me wrong: my best friends made my divorce about them too. I was no longer invited to the Gap senior merchandising executives' homes for dinner or camping near the songbird sanctuaries of Point Reyes with the Marin kids or to Ultra Nectars Oakland warehouse raves.

We were reacting all over the place, starting first with me. Negative thinking created a negative mirror for me at myself! As Mr. Chopra, should have reminded me at this time, I was binge drinking my self-importance because of what happened. The more I thought of my life and what it wasn't, the more misunderstood I became. My thoughts were not improving my life. When break ups happen, we subconsciously create a shell of defensive, petty hell for ourselves. I told the same story for years! It's pettiness at its best.

During that time, my career was as erratic as usual, but that is normal for me. I simply kept on going to have something happen instead of nothing.

I got a sales job (killing it on the hundreds of phone calls every day from Palo Alto) while developing Hula Sisters boutique swimwear line. I was working non-stop! I was selling cotton candy bunny bikinis to Nolan's on the Wharf in Santa Cruz, and placed a 5K order with Dianne's Swimwear of San Diego. Sales were the perfect wave rider for me because I made more money with less self-loathing and administrative mistakes.

my embarrassment, my ego

I was left with myself. I was left to write my adventure and make new friends. My departed had campaigned for himself and up coming wife, with old and new friends to prepare them that a new wife was now in my place. It happens all of the time. I could sit at home and crumble under the television's fear or go out and get one shittier job. Shitty jobs are better than no job! No matter how dull --I learn something about myself. On a dimmer note, my inner dialogue, however, was exhausting because it was self-importance at its best. Our ego is embarrassed because we made the wrong choice in the first place.

We can agree that when we get divorced it's been a long time coming. Let's not fool ourselves that it is any other way. Despite the unquestionable detachment on so many levels after the six years together, I contributed to the demise. I was always talking, not listening and sucking the energy out of the room over nothing and what I was going to do. The Bay Area's community is a highly sophisticated and progressive place. The people that relocate there have education and promising careers. Our friends from SF by way of Minnesota, Wisconsin, and Westport, Connecticut rarely said anything of my self-absorbed or childlike stories. They gave me the grace to listen to my bullshit. They wanted to see me be quiet, I'm sure. They were satisfied in their growing careers and holistic lives.

My friends in SF by way of Babylon, NY (the best ever) encouraged my dancing jiggling, feather boa slinking ways, which was hot at 34 years old. For most of that marriage, I believed I deserved adoration, affection, and praise without giving enough to receive the gifts I was asking for. I thought this husband should show me much more love and I imagine he wished I were a broader and strategic thinker. This husband #1 was my first glimpse of insincerity that made him a passive aggressive person. What he says and what he does is not the same thing. If you are not used to it, it punches you hard in the face. Right you guys? Oh god. Passive aggressive people have a hard time expressing their feelings; especially their feelings toward people with dominant personalities (like mine).

In love I was looking on outside for approval (I still do its pathetic), and seeking superiority instead of going within for peaceful calm. Always! The idea of this marriage (good luck with that one) was disguising my inferiority complex and further nurturing my quick stunt with co-dependency. Nothing feels worse than co-dependency. Yikes.

I was devastated, but during that marriage, I wanted to do what I wanted to do, see my self-importance? So that is what I got! I may have acted like I cared about my marriage, but I really did not. I was more important than my marriage. My ego refused to see the warning signs. It was protecting me and softening the blow of rejection. This relationship had a two-year decline into nothingness.

Does this sound familiar, everyone?

My father rejected me unintentionally like all parents, but this cut was the deepest because of who I was, what I deserved, and what I expected from the universe. Expectations of others are future resentments, just saying'. During the final eggshell days with him, I remember not shouting or being enraged even when my marriage felt so distant, I would not dare because then I would get more silent treatment.

I am an agreeable person when things go my way, but when they don't; I spiral downward with dim thoughts and negative discussions about other people.

You too?

Friends and family do not want to hear about the troubles associated with the failure of this union. After many months of soothing our broken hearts (egos) they want nothing to do with your bad or sad feelings. I had to manage my feelings of rejection and grow from the choice that I made. I thought I would never get over my ego's feelings of embarrassment. But I asked myself again, "What were you doing with this guy in the first place?"

divorce town

"self-importance causes unhappiness in marriage. Then you get divorced. It's a simple formula."

\- kkshaw47

Once the shock wore off I was anxious about what my own shadow would do and how I would manage financially. For three months after this Oracle sales rep escorted himself down to Menlo Park, to live, I sat on my couch with a brightly lit skylight and watched multiple reruns of vintage Behind The Music. My brother Tom would call me every other morning from the east coast, and remind me. To 1) get a job 2) go to the gym and 3) expect that you have to be prepared for life's ups and downs because they are coming! I only hope I can help him in his abyss as he helped me. Soon, though, my girlfriends gave me a couple of tickets to paradise (Santa Cruz) and I began to make friends with the abyss, again, but now on a higher level of risk and uncertainty.

This is when you realize that being single is fun. There were Healdsburg parties to crash, raves in Bolinas and Black Eyed Pea gigs (pre-Fergie) to attend. As I mentioned earlier, I started to work as a prospector in Palo Alto and enjoyed sales because I was generating my own intensity. I began to have fun with working full time in sales, peddling my homegrown swimwear Hula Sisters around to boutiques on the weekend, and going out with people who were single.

Through the fun I had a broken ego. I did not heal properly from the rejected feelings that put me in jeopardy of paying a high debt to the universe. That means that my perspective of anyone and anything was skewed. I was not operating from a place of pure truth, which was how I was feeling would be the type of person I'd attract.

See this karma?

Underneath any new relationship (soon after a challenging split) there is rage, resentment and disappointment. The new love interest that is being lured into this sexy web is not aware of the "inside" and it is not fair to anyone. The bitter and continual complaining set me up for failure in the next relationship that was supposed to take me to a better place. It was a poor choice (my own), not the new shiny boyfriend I was meant to have.

Was I hung over from chaos, choices and self-important behavior? Maybe.

ego's deceptive ways

I had great friends during this marriage. We had the most civil and delightful dinner parties under the stars of Shell Ave in Mill Valley. These were Christina's dear friends and they did love me. The problem was, I did not love me, so how could I reciprocate? I had a difficult time getting over the friend break ups. I was ego pulling the friend card all day long.

Christina and Jim began a friendship with his new wife and family. We have to let people do whatever they want to because they do! It felt far worse than losing the husband! I went on and on about, look what happened to me. It was so boring. My best friend and her family do not love me anymore. The point was that I was trying to control other people, which is unproductive. I was full of self-loathing, which we all know does not bring out the best in us. "Look at that has happened to me." "Look at how terrible that was." I would conclude, "He gave me no money." If I was not saying it, I was thinking it.

What kind of results was this approach manifesting? Yikes, I needed to let go of self-importance!

I was always sincere enough, but I thought I deserved more from the universe. There is an upside to ego. My ego propelled me to create and sell Hula Sisters on the weekend, get on the phones earlier to dial up the east coast to pitch data cleansing & analytics software. I worked hard then, but my ego (not I) was broken. Ego broken means, comparing myself to everyone in my way, shit talking about the departed hubby, his friends, our friends, etc. The more I complained about losing my friends, the worse my situation seemed to become. Do you see karma here? I do! I was doing all of the right things but not feeling, thinking or being them.

For example, when our partners leave us, and they made that decision, you and I are left holding the mirror of ourselves. Our marriages disintegrated because we chose a person we were incompatible with, or worse, we did not water a perfectly good relationship enough. We wanted to be like everyone else.

That is exactly what I did, twice. People, events, children, sex, money and characters' affect our marital relationships as we grow into adulthood. We are very different from the life span of 30 to 40 to 50 to 100 years old! Accepting our choices and living with them in a graceful way, is the key to life, right?

During this time, I believe I became less sincere than any time before or after.

Hmm, again, do you think my ego was deceiving me with thoughts and actions that were manifesting less than a perfect future? My homemade ego ale was selling out and it was seemingly tasty, but I always wanted more than I could handle!

Chapter 4

ego black out: drinking my self-importance

During this time, I could not understand how the universe turned on me. I was on a rampage of non-stop shit talking of what the universe did to me! In that powerful upsetting and lesson-learning period, I found more dimly lit thoughts and more complaining.

I was disappointed on the path I was on because snowdrifts and all night dancing were fraying the single girls club. I did get stronger from working full time and trying to design and develop a boutique swim line --all while kissing snowboarders and farmers in western Marin. I had to have a plan so I would not fall down into no work and no money.

In July 1999 a fiery Sean Penn type of guy came to SF for a date that lasted four years. He was a local guy from NY, Italian and Irish descent with the brightest smile you have ever seen. We dated and very soon after purchased a fix upper in Bernal Heights. This was a big task for wimpy, I really want something for nothing, me.

His not quite A-lister tirades flared up from multiple Heinekens. We were the happiest people on the block from the outside. Everyone admired our costly investment and construction of an Edwardian style house right on top of Coleridge Street, our bikini company, and our work ethic. In the beginning, we had a revolving door of people over to the house (construction zone) for beers and dinner. We had one of the best neighbors in the world, Henry Velázquez. To this day he is a person I admire because of his gentle heart and sincerity, while screaming up the SF hillside on his loud death bike. He was fierce and always found peace no matter what chaos was going on in his family life, the neighborhood or the world.

Sean and I endured a difficult relationship for three out of the four years. It was a hard place emotionally because I was so pissed off that the Silicon Valley sales rep abandoned me and my infant ego was screaming at the universe for not providing me- everything.

During the months of building our house on the hill, traveling to Mexico for weddings in Cabo, New Year's Eve parties in The Castro, snowboarding in Lake Tahoe, Jamie Lerner's Raves (the CTO of XUMA), I continually sat in my kitchen, talked on the phone and drank coffee while discussing ways in which I deserved more and more and more.

At that time, I was working either full time selling integration & network services or taking the 1800 SelectQuote calls to contribute to the real estate investment with money.

It takes more than money to conquer a fixer-upper and that is elbow and kneecap grease. My ego was fully loaded back then. Mr. Penn and I worked really hard and we partied harder. We were both broken hearted from life and furious with the universe, which meant one another.

We always had fun despite the fear and rage between us. We day danced at Kelly's Mission Rock's Second Sunday in 2001. It was the most fun day ever! We went house boating in Lake Shasta in June of that summer, to Mexico for Dianne and Don's Wedding on March 5th 2001, we terrorized the Monkey Bar by feeling roofied by Cosmopolitans. We probably were roofied. My best friends from Babylon were concerned about me during this time; they loved me despite my fucking asshole ego, tweaking hard partying ways and volatile relationship. I created this reality with my driven ego, my continual shit talking (the worst) and my reactive behaviors. I was blacking out all over the place from my bad choices and unhappy attitude. Still!

In the end, this east coast Sean Penn and I were incompatible. I invested in a costly construction job that we single-handedly finished in two years, which was amazing. But his fiery rage was always present, no matter who was in his path. I hung on to this toxicity because I did not have the strength to go anywhere else. I became conditioned to his yelling and screaming late at night, which was very hurtful to my own self-esteem.

From the beginning, my self-importance got me in trouble here, right?

We really had one adventure after another in the total of four years together. The moments were difficult, but the memories were fond.

Our fun at times was--edgy to say the least.

We went to Visalia, hometown of the Sierra Mountains and partied with film motion picture catering giants, there were rattlesnakes everywhere, so strange! That peaked my great fear of snakes that weekend. We went seal watching to San Luis Obispo (it was so gorgeous) and at the same time bike riding through the organic wineries. We drove beside big wheels and motor crossers in Pismo Beach and we camped in Soda Bay CA with mullet biker people. It was the adventure that kept on giving.

I was embarrassed by the dysfunction of this relationship. I found ways to defend his screaming at me in public, or his inexcusable behavior after multiple Kelly green bottles. His ego spent (and probably still does) a lot of time defending his infantile behavior. It protected him on occasion, but I don't think he will survive unless he loses this destructive shield. His ego fakes him out!

Sorry, honey, it's this way for all of us.

He could lash out with fire and rage when things did not go his way. Friends picked up on our dysfunction soon in our relationship and ran for the hills or watched in horror. My soul was aching.

I was still furious with the universe and really looking for him to make everything better, even though his heart was broken too. See me looking on the outside for comfort again? Most of this relationship was on autopilot. It means it is on life support, both of you know it. There were many things that were wrong with us, yet I made the choice to spend time with him. What the hell was wrong with me? Low self-esteem or co-dependency, I suppose. It's the oldest story in the book.

The vision for my birthday was to stay in Monterey during the sunny, happy, golden month of September. We settled in the foggy socked beachfront hotel. We planned to hike up to dinner and walk back by way of the coastal shore and watch the birds go to sleep in their nests! This was the path until one taste of Napa's best red grape too many. We were getting ready for my delicious birthday dinner at the Monterey Inn. We had a very fun party in our surf side beach room. We were whooping it up, laughing, playing music and getting ready for the edge as always. I remember these particular trees and a foggy wind in Carmel and Monterey like the movie, Play Misty For Me, (the Fatal Attraction film of the 70's with Clint Eastwood and Jessica Walters). Maybe it is because of the awful movie of destructive love. The sun shines brightly in the Bay Area but the fog hangs hard in the city during the months of July and August. It's creepy strange. It's the winter in the summer.

As we walked down the stairs of this Inn, I recall feeling overly wobbly from my allergy to festive spirits. When I am very lit, I show it better than anybody! I was trying to act normal, but it was beyond my control. I was going down, no one else.

Fade to black.

I woke up much later that night, in my clothes (thank god) in our room. Joe comes blazing through the door with a police officer. I remember thinking: we were just having a nice little birthday party here! What happened? He is yelling at me as loudly as possible with blood covering his entire face. I am thinking, weren't we just at dinner?

I suppose, just after our festive dinner, Joe tucked me in bed, and headed toward the beach. Thank goodness he did not drag me out there too. He approached a gathering at a beach fire and "said" that this particular group of cockroaches jumped him. With that many Heinekens there is always an element of lying or denial. Drunk people will make up any story to get the blame off them. He chose the wrong group to piss off – because they jumped him and kicked his ass, bloody. He often went out after twenty cans or more. I am not exaggerating – twenty!

No matter what happened the night before, it was someone else's fault. Or better, I had to agree with him (that it was my fault) so he could regain his reality. This was disturbing to me. He's a good guy, but his ego is dismal. It has hurt him so many times.

That morning was shattering, not to mention that we had to nurse his cuts, bruises, and ego. Of course we had to fill out a police report against these strangers, which I bet did nothing wrong. And I was sick from sadness towards myself, but again helpless to do anything about what was happening in my life.

The more I blamed and resented him, the more it came back to me with a force. We had a costly investment in a big Victorian home on top of a hill overlooking the Bay Bridge and not in a spiritual place of love. We stood beside one another, trying to understand the off-center world we had created for ourselves. This meant more southern California active sport trade shows, more trips back East, a New Years celebration down to Cabo San Lucas, more super blizzards and less friends to hang around with. People were tiring of the KK and crazy boyfriend show because at any moment, it could explode into nasty fire flames. Do you know what I mean?

did my thoughts get me here?

Look what my ex (my choice) did to me? Look at this volatile (my choice) boyfriend I have? I was spending time thinking about others' actions and discussing what they should be doing, etc. How did I go from having so much to this? I had fewer friends, no community, no beautiful children to love and no real money. Thinking beyond this current mess of a relationship, I needed a job again, had to build a household from scratch, and find a way to be happy in manic chaos.

what the universe owed me (sigh)

The ego has a very hard edge sword to defend itself. The more I defended my choices or myself, the less control I had.

My silly ego got me into an unfit marriage to begin with. I always ask, what was I doing with him in the first place? Women are totally awesome, but we are so naive that we give our power, money, confidence, sex, love, and understanding to men! WTF it's bad out there ladies. I don't believe men actually want such a responsibility and or they don't know what to do with so much natural, raw, solution seeking, intuitive, emotional and sincere power!

> *"I continued to drink my self-involved homemade ale which was love me, take care of me, do what I want, and say what I want you to say. Of course the universe was going to bite me!"*
>
> —kkshaw47

What is the marriage epidemic all about? When we separate, who is doing whom a favor? It seems egocentric and cowardly at the same time. Everyone wants to fit in to society, I did it to fit in. In the US we have education and work opportunities in the workplace. Why do we get married so early? How do we feed our souls & curiosity with years of love, success and failure to be the humble and sexy partner everyone is looking for? At 31 years old I would have lost the charming wife medal because I was self-involved! I continued to drink my self-involved homemade ale which was love me, take care of me, do what I want, and say what I want you to say.

Of course the universe was going to bite me!

As my self-importance was peaking and our egos were yelling at the top of our lungs "What about me?" I got nothing. He was looking right at me saying the same thing. The more I yelled and demanded, so did he!

See how it works, everyone? Why couldn't he understand what I wanted? Why wasn't he listening to me?

Blaming others is a waste of time. I criticized him for being mean and destructive when he was having a bad day. He could be difficult, but I chose to be with him. My Nick Cage looking husband left me and I had nothing better to do than avoid the truth. I was miserable because I wanted to talk about what I deserved all of the time. I spoke often of what the universe was supposed to deliver (sigh).

When you get down to the pitfalls of ego, you are pushed to go within for responsibility.

I met Susan Sparks during this time thank god. Susan was married to David Stone; a super duper fun Manhattan guy I met post marriage. I love and adore Susan Sparks. She is the most profoundly spiritual being I have ever met who taught me the most basic life skills of anyone. I guess it is mindfulness and self-awareness. She should be writing all of these ideas, not me.

Just for the record everybody, Susan Sparks is the friend who referred to all of her loved ones as <u>lamb</u>. I did not come up with this affectionate word on my own. Right, Sue?

So one late spring day on top of Coleridge Street, Susan and I were having our partners are assholes conversation, even though we picked them. She was a woman adored by men for her sweet disposition and light green eyes. She wanted David to respect, love and understand her feelings, good or bad. It was that simple. And on the phone that day up on the hill, we are getting down and dirty about her sometimes selfish, husband and my temper tantrum boyfriend. That afternoon, in my off blue kitchen, call it intuition, guardian angels or gut (all same) – I said to Susan, "I do not do a God damn thing here (in this house) except bring home checks, talk on the phone and complain about what the world should be doing for me."

The words and feelings found me. Does that make sense?

I convinced myself that I was working to pay for groceries

or wine or weekend trips. But "enough" was not making for a joyful house to build, even if we were not going to be together, ever. Do you think that is my crazy ego again? Bringing me unhappiness?

I continued to Susan on the telephone that day, "This relationship will not end up in happiness, but I am going to give it all I have as a person (within reason). I will bake a blueberry crisp for him and I will stop being reactive to his negativity, which I was. It can't hurt, right? I will help him with any difficult project that I do not want to get dirty doing. I am going to go to Home Depot at midnight if we need to." The egocentric energy literally left me.

Here comes the light.

It was like I became present in one moment.

Is this what mindfulness is supposed to be like?

I thought that this then partner should fix our emotional problems for us, for me, because I am so sincere and deserving right? See me looking for only the glitz and glamour here? When we continually look to others for our happiness or sadness, we go nowhere. When we get down to the pitfalls of ego, we have no choice but to go inside for responsibility. I realized that I should be changing, but how was I going to do that?

baby carriage with ab & tj - the best! 1964

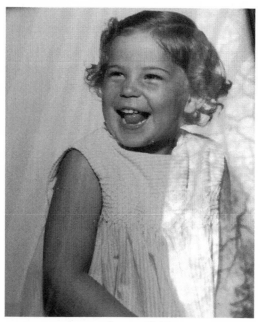

me happy, 1966

family photo harbour island bahamas, 1972

the big adventure to harbour island, bahamas 1972

babylon sisters, 2016

brady, 2011

brady & daddy, 2012

momzillas, 2016

me

Section 4

letting e go

Chapter 5

letting go to be in control

Making my own happiness meant getting over myself pronto! I felt like a changed person, immediately. This was not a codependent "hope we get better" situation. This was doing what was asked of me within reason! I stopped reacting to the difficulty of this situation (for the most part, not always).

I needed to be a business partner, friend, and contribute to the colossal construction of this house. My mantra became, with this relationship that would never thrive, "*I will keep on keeping on, it will never be right. If I am in the present here and trying to be helpful, what could go that wrong?*" There was going to be a reward at the end for us but, many times it was a grind with him and I should have left. I got over myself and did what I said I was going to do. I tried! I went to the industrial supply store and carried heavy cement bags up three flights of stairs. He blissed with me with a flower garden on top of our adobe brick patio on top of the hill in Bernal Heights! It was a garden on top of a mountain! It was magical. Caring for the flowers, shrubs and our dwarf lemon tree made me happy. We changed for the better immediately. We became kinder as human beings and not boyfriend and girlfriend! In the end he manipulated the sale of the house money out of me. He's rich now because of me and it's ok because I am free!

Does our healthy, selfless, love for each other build trust? Is that right? Does self-importance cause unhappiness even with the best intentions? Why are we drawn to partnerships with our self-importance untamed at all? Are we looking to receive more than to give? On some level we must be because I was. In my deserving candor, I was expecting more praise, more understanding, more money, more freedom, more negative discussions that involved me, more attachment to others, more comparing myself to look better or worse. I was not in a state of loving of others. I thought others should love me more. Isn't that funny? It's the truth. I was still prone to rage caused by reactive behavior, when ignited.

Fire!

I did not realize until later that family life; being super humbled, loving someone, and taking care of others from a place of strength is a blend of bliss. More please!

being happy in chaos

> *"children and teenagers and are <u>exempt</u> because they need ego to grow and explore."*
>
> - kkshaw47

At that time, my career was unsuccessful, and I was feeling helpless to my cognitive disorder and having poor radar with romance. One year before my 40th birthday, I thought I would never be in love again, I had that chance already and forget children. I have to make certain that I am a happy person. The most important thing for me at this time was my strong wonderful ego family and sincere friendships, grounding me.

My hard-core ego could have come from growing up in the 70's, sitting beside my parents' inevitable chaos & my

ADD causing me to detach from what I could not understand (still don't). Perhaps throughout my life I have been feeling lost and frustrated and not having any way to communicate how it made me feel anxious and unsure. Accepting life on my parents' terms was one of the biggest lessons for me. I respect, love and adore them for their imperfections! They are so delightful! The great part of childhood is you learn to live with "what is." It certainly does not have to be like that forever either. Throughout life perhaps it was my ego that drove me to the countryside of France, or the unbearable hike into the Kalalau Valley or the cryptic trance house raves in French Caribbean and Northern California. It helped me tumble through a world that I do not understand on others' terms, only my own. Sorry if I do not understand you, if my eyes become glazy, I have ADD and it's terrible! ADD also helped me accept my fate in life. I couldn't be the best, but I could work wonders with what the spirit had given me. Cheers to trying!

Teenagers and children are also exempt from this warning label because they need ego to grow and explore. The kids and young adults have to find their fierce friends, duke it out, take the wild carpet ride, sing in the musical, speak out for others, fall in true love, go snowboarding & surfing, start a band and build a new infrastructure to remove plastic pollution! We use our egos to make our dreams come true!

Yikes, who cares? The global family we share is genius, scientific, shrewd, proud, devastated, courageous, healing, calculating, and building all - for countries, states, and communities. Our global family is strategic. The ego could be disrupting our human existence at the moment. Adults can turn off the egos, leave it to the children & young adults who deserve their self-importance, they need it to grow. If we let go of self-importance we can get back to building a better place for others.

The petty mud slinging with wannabe Sean Penn (he was a lot like him) was the depth of my ego hangover and failure to connect with others. I was turning 40 and there was no more statues to knock down, no more people to blame, no one else to tell the story of look what happened to me? There was only space and air to get a deep breath and slowly, very slowly, let it out. I think I was so afraid at that time. I was not hopeful about going home after the sale of the Coleridge Street house. Again I was sad not to be more successful in marriage or my career. I knew that I would keep going for the job and life. I was going to live with my parents. Get ready for this one!

When I was still in California, the brightest blue Forget Me Not flower in the garden, Jackie Navarro, from Casper, Wyoming once told me to write down an affirmation or prayer or what you want to visualize in your mind and "pray on it" everyday.

The affirmation said, "Please God/universe bring me home to the pine evergreen trees close to the ocean. Please let me find a wonderful partner who loves me for who I am who would like to have a family with me." I put it in my lingerie/sock drawer and reflected on it maybe five times, 'cause I forgot all about it, ADD right? Who forgets to read their affirmation?

Leaving California brought back all the losses and my disconnect from Christina Pettigrew, one of my closest friends ever. If anyone was going to hurt because I was rejected back then it was going to be her. Losing friendships is the most difficult part of divorce. My low self esteem (which were expectations; future resentments, total bullshit on my part) brought more anger and resentment into my life, which I did not need. I was profoundly sad for leaving the friendships, because I was a social butterfly turned back into a lonely caterpillar. The reason that I had lost my friendships in Cali was that I did little to nurture them. It was all about me, somehow.

Christina and Jim are a wonderful love story. I was there for one of the first times they kissed under the stars in East Hampton, NY; I was the maid of honor on the Peking at the South Street Seaport in 1989. I understand Christina Pettigrew very well. We were (are) very close yayas, it's how the stars aligned us, and I am smart enough to know that.

I had to blame Christina for abandoning me. She thought I abandoned her. We did not speak for a little over a year maybe. See how this works? I had to be angry at someone, so how about your best friend in the world who became friendly with your ex husband and his new sparkly wife? Jim was and still is a great friend of not quite Nick Cage. Good for them, right? It happens all of the time.

forgiveness is a relief!

My "look what happened to me" story with Christina, (a tall mid summer magenta pink colored flower in my garden) went on for a long time; it was exhausting for my friends and family to hear. She called me so many times during this period. I would not forgive her.

After the fifth or sixth call, I asked the wise and heavenly Susan Sparks, "Sue, should I forgive her?"

And she said, "She sure is trying."

Dear friends convinced me to speak with Christina and let it go! I realized that I loved Christina more than I disliked my x-Man, and it felt great, immediately.

I gave myself the green light to forgive her and it was a relief. Again, my friendships served as my family for many years. I was lucky.

At that stage of my life close to the wise age of 40, I was realizing that unhappiness was due to my thoughts and actions and self-fueled ego. It was time to really let the self-centered, attention seeking, and easily flattered, defensive, side of my self-go.

It was a relief because I was less hung over from self-importance!

Good-bye, bitch!

By my 40th birthday, we were getting ready to sell 79 Coleridge Street. I was fragile (broken ego and cognitive challenges again here). I was in charge of the sale transaction of Coleridge Street. There were residual feelings of anxiety with my love life and career, and our house was not selling, of course. We tried to sell it for a good six months. We had a three-bedroom on the block for 825K or something ridiculous. But it was prime real estate with a crystal clear view of the Bay Bridge. After twelve years of adventure and fun, SF was not working for me. On a whim, with a BFF, chirping on the phone, I decided to move back to Long Island with my family and start over. I guess I was listening to my intuition then.

In August 2003, I flew home, got an Ann Taylor dress, walking shoes and a job as a sales rep for The NY Sun in Tribeca, NY.

Once we did sell 79 Coleridge Street, we both were free to move on. I remember feeling warmth towards Sean, for teaching me life lessons (with an iron fist) of understanding and behavior towards any person. We were friends (always were really) after all was said and done. He drove the monster four-wheeler back to NY with my belongings, his Harley Davidson and Corvette! I am very grateful to Sean (and my sweetheart best friend Laurie) for taking my things back home that summer!

I took my failures to heart, but, gradually, my thoughts

turned to hope because there was no one to blame anymore. I continued to put my misguided ego in its place. I recited my hopeful desires from my affirmation (ripped piece of paper) in my lingerie drawer and began to focus on what I thought a great marriage, life, community could be.

The breakup and chaos with the fellows in SF was an important path to my awakening. I had to turn inside out to get back to who I wanted to be, not was. I was completely hung over from my life choices.

My newly homemade ego ale with a strong shot of humility --the best I have ever had!

letting go of what I deserved

Learning calm in the chaos meant the universe owed me nothing. It meant letting go of "a story" in life that will prevent me from an emotionally happy place.. I have so much to be thankful for. Everything you could dream of, I have, and this is before Toddy.

I was letting go of what I thought I deserved from the universe and others. I let it go of my failed romance, my dreams, what I deserved, and I was fine. I had the ability to walk, thank you Buddha and I had a family that would provide me love and warmth. How lucky was I? I even had another sales job, right?

I was happy to be standing on my own two feet, I had no control and I was very good with it. I was feeling Zen stillness. I was somehow breathing better in smoggy Long Island of NY and I was somehow more calm and still. I was accepting life in a positive way. Imagine an egomaniac, like me and what I deserved?

Uncertainty was still on the horizon though; don't let the calm fool you.

Once I returned to NY, I was right back to work in the city. A new place again. The autumn moon greeted me each morning as I hoofed it to the train. I pounded the pavement to and from Chambers Street at *The New York Sun*.

I was delighted to have my parents as roommates. They are well read on literature, news, politics, entertainment, art, and sports. They inhale the news and television all day long. My head is way more in the clouds than my family.

Our family used to party with the Henrys on Christmas Day and in the backyard under the 70's summer stars. Henrys, whose father was District Attorney of Suffolk County and also a police detective with five strawberry blonde haired children, all with very polite sweetness about them.

The youngest child (a twin) of this unique and American Scottish family is - Maggie. She is one of my great spiritual guides, a fairy godmother, which she really does not believe me yet. She married (in 1999) the quiet, dapper, younger brother of Todd, Bradley. On Halloween Eve, she invited my parents and I to an autumn pumpkin party for all of the kids. She asked me if I remembered her brother in law, Todd Shaw:

"You remember, from Amityville, right?"

I said, "Yes, how is he?"

"Well, he is fine and awesome and living in NYC," Maggie, said with her Scottish bow tie of a smile.

I didn't really think that much about it because my Virgo ways make me very particular in my attraction to men. I left the orange-lit jack o lantern party that balmy, wet October day thinking, Is Maggie going to be at the country club with her family and Todd? Fall's colors reminded me of a rainbow.

I was in a happy state of mind helping and doing for others; it felt like a very good use of my time. I probably did later to my family unconsciously what they may have done in me earlier. I was delighted to care for my parents once I lost my own self-importance. Any day that I could drive them somewhere, help my father with his Rotary responsibilities, go shopping, take out the garbage, help friends with their parents or kids, I was happy to do so.

I thought further, no matter what happens that is unfavorable I am going to let it go and be happy where I am. So many people understand this 100%, but I did not.

At the New York Sun, back in NYC, I thought the sales pit would be grey and creepy, like a super Republican/conservative and just dreary. It was, it sucked so badly. But as usual the sales pit was filled with one funny and interesting character after another. Our competitor was *The New York Post*. I was out there calling Miss Kate Hart at The Ritz Carlton and the ad agencies who represent the Plaza while trying to sell a quarter page for 5K.

Anything to get recognized! Oh boy, so hard, though, if your product or service is not #1 or #2.

Hold on, I'm having an ego moment here.

reset button

The reason I did not make my sales number, is because I did not engage with my prospects enough to turn them into clients. I do not believe I made my number even once at *The Sun*. I could not bring that shit home! I am so sorry!

I still felt hopeful and happy. Being with old friends and their children and families felt so good! I was glad to be alive and detached from what I thought my life should be.

That November, I was delighted to be at Thanksgiving dinner with my family at Southward Ho Country Club.

Sure enough, while I'm drinking my soda during cocktail hour, in comes Todd Shaw at 40 years old.

He was a silver bullet waltzing through the Thanksgiving

Day happy hour crowd at the country club! He was cuter than when I remembered him from 15 years old, when he was a little chubby and shy. Sorry, Toddy, had to say it. And now he had all of this experience, and he was not 15 years old, passing me a Marlboro and can of Budweiser. He was a grown man and quite sure of himself. I was just in from The West Coast and he lived in So Ho and I was like, oh, boy how cool are you with your silver hair now? I had pheromones for Todd Shaw that I thought would never be, my Virgo way, I suppose. I was surprised, but I figured, well, if it was good, even with a fiancé of a ladybird on his shoulder, then maybe we could be great friends. He worked at Smith Barney, he lived on Charleston Street and he asked me to a party for a CRT benefit! I was excited to go and hoped he would call, and he didn't. I was like, oh, cool, 'cause he does have a fiancé (which does not faze me because of the West Coast) and we all know how it works, and we can be great friends. I was certain that he had cool friends too!

I went back to my family's table of howling laughter; we ate the turkey (poor little turkey) like Vikings, and got ready to head out the door. We were standing on the stairs of the club, all 11 of us, and just as we were snapping a family photo, up walked Todd Shaw, Vice President at Smith Barney and gave me his business card. I was left standing there and my family was grinning at me, but then all shook it off and said, "Smile!"

After a good month or so Todd put a call into my parents house. My mother, father and I did the happy dance, I am sure. That following week we met just before New Year's at the Town Bar. When we sat down on the couch at Town, I asked what have you been doing, blow by blow, since we were 15 years old?

"Boating, skiing in Aspen, running the NYC marathon, and cultivating my career here in NY at Smith Barney. "

I replied. "Selling term life insurance, selling my newly developed boutique swimwear line, recovering from a bitch slap of a divorce and just closed a monumental San Franciscan Victorian renovation."

Looking back we both agreed that this was going to be a good story, friends or not. Soon after he had parted with his lady and we began a very sexy friendship. During this time, I had learned to remove my destructive ego from romance as well. Seriously! Perhaps it was my childhood, or my father, but I could be a Jack Russell terrier when it came to what I deserved in romance. But a dramatic divorce (thank you) and another very failed relationship (that I signed up for) humbled me. We had such great fun as friends and discovered we were great tantric partners. Yahoo! In between his leaving her and the new thing with me, I knew he had a menu to taste the awesome women of NY. I couldn't blame him. Removing my ego in this circumstance worked out well. Partners can feel and do what they want. They have to want to be with and love you. This is a law of the universe, right?

I realized that removing my self-importance could work. When we parted for a "brief" time, I said, to his surprise, I want to be close to you and I feel you need to get your "sexy" on with others. There were no worries either.

All I know is that we were best friends and having a dating blowout. We enjoyed lots of sexy cocktails and pinot noir at dinners. Oh, it was the best! We hosted roof top parties at the Thompson Hotel during Soho's Summer solstice. We had fondue at his parents' bayside home right in West Islip with picnic checkered nametags and sprigs of herbs.

We were drinking Provencal rose, and kissing at Raoul's on Prince Street.

Round of Secretinis anyone?

One happy shining day in September 2003, we were preparing for a loft party with Todd's neighbors, Ben and Aimee. Ben and Aimee were the Ropers from Three's Company! They were his landlords and our dear friends. I will never forget their flair, spirit and heartfelt laughter. I returned home from a Friday after work and found rose petals all over his apartment. Todd had a twinkle in his eye and I was like, oh, he loves me, that is so dear and I am so happy, yahoo!

Todd was always in his navy blue Brooks Brothers shirt and white Calvin Klein boxer shorts during those days, which I will always cherish.

From the doorway of our apartment, I saw a tiny light blue box on his bed. I opened the pretty little box and saw a necklace chain that is the style of that year.

He carefully took it out and put it around my neck and said, "I want you to be my best friend forever."

I was way over the moon to be friends forever! The September sunlight blinded me again and I blinked up and then down to see Todd Shaw on one knee, his eyes more piercing blue than the azure little box he was holding. I take the box, open it slowly, and out pops out a starred flowered snowflake of a diamond engagement ring!

I knew we had a great time, but he took me by surprise. I said yes, yes and we were ready to drink that strong Law of Attraction together.

One day he said to me, "I drew you to me like a magnet. You are the first girl I ever had a crush on. "You are the woman I always dreamed of, I knew it from the start."-Firefly *the secret is not real; manifesting sure is fun!*

Was it the affirmation from my lingerie drawer? Did my thoughts manifest this dream come true? Absolutely not, but it sure felt like it. To this day, the Law of Attraction is making me tipsy. Being married is made up of gifts to cherish, a garden to tend to or bake like your favorite birthday cake! Some days are better than others! I chose to be in a partnership and I was going to get over myself to create happiness no matter what.

How on earth did this happen? Perhaps from the power of myths, hopeful risks, easy tragedies, lots of failure, letting go, being in the moment and the power of my thoughts that drew my marriage and then my baby Viking into my life?

self-importance creates divorce

I was very excited to get the chance to marry again. I had always hoped for happy love, right? Why do we have marriages of such unrest? It could start with self-importance. It potentially ruins every marriage. I swear you have to get married after 35 for ladies and 40 for men. I believe for a long while I had this perception of love that felt like, how much love can you give or show to me? I withheld so many feelings that should have been revealed and it was boring to love me. I have a great fear of rejection. God forbid, KK, right? Then if you have the gift of caring about your partner (and not what you deserve from them), you learn to love with only kindness with zero agenda attached. Imagine!

setting up the laws of marriage

See why I'm drinking the "Is love happiness or is happiness love drink"?

Todd brings this idea up a lot; I am so glad that he listened to me.

He often says, "She said to me on top of the Gansevoort Hotel, if you ask me to do anything within reason, I will do it. And if I ask anything from you (within reason) then you have to do it for me."

He will always say, wow, that's a good one? I think we have both decided that it can build trust immediately. It is the best! I hooked lined and sunk this yummy Wall Street number in a NY minute that late sunny afternoon.

We got married in the Church of Incarnation on November 20, 2004 with a festive party following at Loft 11. It was the best day ever.

We held on to one another and dove right into the heart of our home and family life's champagne bubbly! Bubbles of romance and laughter in our new kitchen on Avon Place with red white and blue fun! While kissing my baby dwarf bunny goodbye, I'd put on my ripped up bright green and orange sneakers to stomp the streets of NYC. We were off to marriage's fun delights with kisses and hugs in our bed all day long. We were hanging up Indian white frames of the Caribbean seas, our vintage color newlywed pictures and more dear and lovely friends, new and old, that we loved to see!

On Monday, January 7, 2008 Brady Thomas was born and we have been bumbling and giggling ever since. He was 8lbs and 13 oz. and with his beauty and happy disposition, he was just about the cutest baby out there. He would smile in his stroller like the happiest baby in the world. This little man brought me down to my knees with thankful gratitude. All parents feel this way. It's such a blessing. There are no words. And Todd is a gift of a husband too. Todd is smart enough to live in the there are no excuses zone, so we can let go and get to the next steps that life is serving us, right? We know it is a wonderful uphill battle. These are the happy times let's get over ourselves already! We could let go of inner complaining and what the universe (person or event) owes us.

Happiness is letting go of what we think our reality should be. That's a good one. We can get over the " story" of self-pity and anger! We can appreciate every moment because we are not consumed with ourselves all day long. Glass of light, crispy no-ego with dinner tonight?

Chapter 6

ego monsters

Now realizing that the universe has delivered the best it knows how, the questions I had for myself were how am I going to manage all of this light and happiness and not suffer an ego relapse? what happens when life is finally put into place and the petty warfare begins, with others? If I am self-unaware, again, then I might miss out on the opportunity of actually being in love and a productive mother! Ha, that is so funny right? At that time, I was convinced that I was ready for the grind, but how should I manage myself in the "normal" society after living in San Francisco for a decade, where everything peculiar, uber unique and progressive is happening? How could I be a great wife and not a reactive infant when I did not get my way? How can I not be a self important and controlling mother where everything is about me? By giving my ego the beat down, while in the line of fire. I was now ordering a glass of light, crispy no-ego to go with the first bites of my delicious dinner! And it was a relief that all of my stories were mostly behind me; I was losing my attachment to everything all at once. You better learn in the suburbs 'cause mothers, fathers and adults have all of this time for passive aggressive petty behavior. There is a lot of "shade" in the suburbs! It is so crazy ego time!

sunset backyard truths fix my ego - pronto

I will always thank Marty Parker, our Amityville neighbor for this exchange, because it taught me a lesson. We were having appetizers at our neighbors' house and early evening cabernets in the boldly flowered dining room and I was telling my story (again) of how my ex-husband left me, and took all of the money, and he is a fucking asshole, can you believe that? Husband #1, way early in the tech boom, had an executive sales job(s) in technology with huge salaries & lucrative stock payouts and more new start-ups to be hired for. Good for him, you know?

Marty looked at me with his twilight vampire chiseled looks and said, "Kristen, did you ever think of how uncomfortable that makes Todd feel, when you continually bring up the story of your ex-husband?"

Marty called me out!

Pause Pause Pause. Yikes.

Marty was suggesting and I was realizing, "I have to end that story beginning right now. Who cares anyway?"

Thank you, Marty Parker, for your honesty and for taking me down exactly when I needed it. He did not think twice about that conversation, but it has had such a good impact on me, because he was so right and luckily I heard it!! I am thankful for others honesty because they see me better than I see myself. I believe that Marty's one statement helped me grow into a new stage of conscious partnering, immediately. It was a shift in one moment. It pushed me into a present, appreciative state of my marriage. It has been working ever since. I stopped narrating my stories of rejection and the story of, can you believe it too? I'd traveled the vortex of familiar, unknown, sadness, ecstasy, abandonment, rejection, anger and removing it from everything I know. I let go of my continual stories, does that make sense? I felt much better about everything.

power of now sparks the truth

During this revelation, I was drinking buckets of coffee and tea in my kitchen. My darling Cindy Sparks and I were in deep conversation on Oprah Winfrey and her spirituality. Cindy tried her best to get all of the girlfriends on the webcast of Eckhart Tolle's <u>New Earth</u>. It seemed amazing, but my ADD and to and from NYC would not allow me to sit down and listen to a webcast/podcast live from Oprah's studio. When I asked her what this was, she simply said, in her smart, matter of fact, targeted way, "The action of removing the ego that fuels reactive behavior, wars and conflict in general that can be eradicated."

I am uncertain if this was verbatim, but that is what I heard and understood on petty behavior and global conflict. Cindy forgets she told it to me this day! Love her.

Yahoo! So letting go of "that story" meant letting go of all the stories! What a relief! Yahoo! So letting go …what a relief. How lucky am I? By now I was proud of my alignment of thoughts, words and actions (towards others) and it tasted delicious!

the no ego blog

I started the no ego blog when Brady was in pre-K. Every moment he was in school I was writing and posting. It was a glimpse of my ideas on the backyard birds, current events and the pitfalls of my self-obsessed behavior! At that time I opened up multiple accounts on twitter and Facebook and enjoyed my first exchange from followers and more importantly, what I learned from them! I found inspiration from social media! I think we all have.

The path to the success of happiness is lucrative. It is splashed all over motivational blogs, FB, twitter, young womens' magazines, television programs, entertainment news, and not regular news. There is a lot of success with books on happiness.

I mean it is so obvious that some of us, most of us, not all of us, are walking around with insincerity that becomes unhappiness! My intuition tells me that insincerity is no path to enlightenment. I am not certain we as a society, or cultural or global family are happy. We cannot get a handle on it because we are self- centered and believe the universe owes us more.

I can be insincere if I believe that someone has betrayed me. Betrayal is part of life. We all go through it. You need sincerity to attract positive energy and true love. It is a good start to a life of friendships that bring out the best in us, with adventure and kindness. Kindness is happiness! We all say we want to be happy, right?

insincerity is closet bullying

Insincerity is sadly acceptable in life and in personal relationships, which is disheartening for me to observe.

Without my friends, I would be lost in the forest trying to understand the other unhappy, egomaniacal lady birds who whisper and laugh at the expense of others. It's a salty strong drink to nowhere! I am beyond disappointed and ashamed how women judge one another just because they are too fearful or lost to face their own realities. Instead they develop alliances of judgment against others for no reason and discuss this at length with everyone but their victim. It's ego coward bullshit. I've observed women exclude other women and children because they are so insincere and fucking envious of everything. It starts with envy I suppose. Their actions are glaringly apparent to everyone. They hide it with a smile and insincerity. Get over your self-importance already, please. I have a big problem with insincerity from others with no legitimate reason at all. It's such an ego move. Do you see my reactive crazy here? My friendships growing up were solid and sincere. I did not have to worry about someone excluding me for <u>no</u> reason at all or talking shit about me when I left the room, (except maybe when I was speaking too loudly at happy hour,) but it never felt insincere. Who started this bullshit insincerity in the first place?

The reason children could bully is because their parents are competitive and resentful assholes and did not have enough sex, far and away travels, rocket ship careers, or random experience in their lives. It is simple. I can see it so clearly. I am glad for my cool friendships in BV 'cause all of the music, the edge, the abyss, the risk, the light, the dark, and the unpredictable, gave us the peace and quiet we need in adulthood, marriage and family.

I do not think it is good karma to talk shit about others actions. It feels so bad to do. We should take a good look at ourselves. Don't we go to church to learn this? When my behavior is bad because I am reactive with Todd in a disagreement, oh God, or I am attaching to others' behavior that I believe are unkind toward me, I become obsessed and self-absorbed. In the past, I never had the time to be a fragile egomaniac during my twenties and thirties 'cause I was traveling, working, getting divorced, moving, and working more to getting hired again.

epidemic of reactive behavior

My reactive crazy behavior is epic in every way. Why are we angry when someone else is angry – 'cause we have nothing else better to do? Reactive behavior is difficult on relationships in general. We are all living in a world of reactive behavior and it feels like we are moving backwards because no one can resolve anything. Our ego will not let us say we are sorry and then let go. We make children say it all of the time! If a family member calls us out on a behavior, don't we know they love us enough to be honest? Do we let them be truthful? It is so important to try and listen to what loved ones are saying that can help, and not lunge into a firestorm of wasteful defensiveness, sigh. I think when others are giving me the truth it is so refreshing and honest and I need to fix it! My ego gets pissed off, don't get me wrong, I am saying fuck off motherfucker in my head, and believe me, the gnarly ego. I want to be loved, so why wouldn't I do what others say within reason? I love that principle very much.

In adulthood, look at how destructive it is. It is hiding in marriage by not letting go of an argument, it does not allow us to hear the truth that we probably should, it does not allow us to let someone tell a story of their own, we chime in and say see me too. The worst of all is that it does not allow us to listen or be sincere.

Insincerity really took me off guard everyone. I was blabbing so much and full of ego I did not realize how angry and insincere the world is! Laugh out loud! Oh my goodness. It's not bringing sunshine and happiness! That's for sure. Insincerity means we genuinely discard other people, its 100% about us. It means we dislike others who have not said one word yet. It is a petty move like no other. I see women trying to dislike other women because they are fashionable, beautiful, sexy or vivacious. We have it so good here in the US. Do you see the appalling prejudice and violence against women in the US? Try Iraq, Syria, Sudan, Nigeria, Zambia, South Africa, Turkey, at the moment? The list is growing out there by the way. Look after your sisters. Women in the world need our help, desperately. And the best we can do is dislike other women who have a better eyelash stylist? WTF! That's a bad joke.

ego in friendship

The ego destroys long time friendships. If we're not conscious of our sincerity, envy, judging, insincerity, reactive behavior in long time relationships, the trust and magic of the friendship will be gone. Why won't our friends let us tell a truth without accepting our apology? We have a delightful long term friendship and one disagreement alters the state of this friendship for the worse, not better? Why do we focus on what others say that is unkind, unfavorable, truths when, for a lifetime they praised us on a daily basis? Truly!

ego in parenting

The state of adoration we express towards our children is breathtaking. It is loving kindness at its best. Why can't we apply this to others? Loving others is a happy state of mind, right? Why can't we transcend our ego and apply this to other family members and friendships (sometimes)? Our ego is a not guiding us to the path of contentment.

I grew up with an imperfect family, (which is perfect for me) and sincere friendships. I am never insincere if I can help it. I am typically (not always) proud of my thoughts of others, which is a gift I give myself, and I am aware when my ego is waiting to take me down, in particular if someone has done me wrong and I slip into a reactive tirade. To be sincere is a goal each day. Please god!

Who cares what our friends do? Who cares what our neighbors do? By the way, our actions are glaring at others. We don't have to speak. Our inaction says it all.

However, if I cannot tell a friend the truth within reason, or you cannot tell me or we are discussing another person's actions at great length, to our own expense, which means we are bored, then what am I doing here? I would rather pick and gather a June jeweled purple and sunshine yellow bouquet of flowers, I call friends, who listen to the truth and take it as a lesson.

accepting apologies without forgiveness

If I love a friend and make a mistake and sincerely apologize, why doesn't it end there? Andy Cohen's Housewives of everywhere are struggling with this petty war on every level. It is sad to watch now. Is insincerity a normal place now? That fact that once dear friends will not accept an apology because they "get off" on their own negative feeling is self-serving at its best. If I say I'm sorry, I mean it. Do we mean it when we say it is okay, but our actions are glaringly apparent to me that you do not forgive me yet? I thought we were supposed to get close as a result of our truths, which is so human. If we think being in negativity with friends and loved ones is right, that is not my mixology, darling. How many hours a day does our mixology of petty ego have us on the telephone to someone who has been listening to this for years, and what all of our friends or loved ones have done to us? I did it for years and years in San Francisco. Oh, that is not a friend if they act that way to me? Do we ever take responsibility for our actions and our thoughts to consider why situations in our life are not ideal? As growing adults in the free world we should be more open to our own truths as life progresses, right?

"the more we judge, the less friends we have." – kkshaw47

I am stunned how we talk shit about others without taking any responsibility for what we've manifested on our own. This is egocentric petty bullshit. If I can drive any point home, it is the fact that we trash our best friends. WTF? Do we know how bad it looks when we say anything judgmental or unkind of our best friend at dinner parties or in passing to others? My heart flinches when I see best friends do this. It is ridiculous and self-serving. Our ego is not fooling anyone. Seriously, I would not judge my best friends. I am always looking for friends, where the ego need not apply. The moment we are discussing other people and listening with judgment, we are screwed. I know I am!

listening without judgment – oh god!

I am surprised how distracted and judgmental I can be while listening to just about everyone, whether I agree or disagree. When I listen with judgment, I am missing out on some new and interesting idea. Does listening with judgment mean, we are unable to listen? Are we comfortable talking at people who are not listening? How could they possibly? It is a monologue from hell. Do we listen only to "up" the person telling the story? Do we listen, with judgment to a completely different story about ourselves? When someone tells us a story we don't even hear it because we are mentally preparing to share our opinion of their story. It goes on and on. Have you seen network news lately? Listening is hard enough and with judgment it is impossible to have genuine conversations. We are enduring insincerity at its best and not having honest trustworthy relationships. It is a huge character defect of mine that I am not going to blame my ADD on for once.

ego monsters

I had a neighbor who maybe unknowingly created an alliance against me. Brady was 100% excluded out of any playgroup, soccer or birthday party that she was involved in. She would say, I love you and Brady so much, but her actions did not match these words at all – sound familiar lambs? It's an epidemic caused by the adults! Her actions were glaringly apparent to me. I am certain that she compares herself to everybody and everything, either she has too much or too little compared to anyone! It causes her great unhappiness! ugh. It is astonishing how seemingly functioning adults get off on the negative things others say. I have never seen such insincerity in my long life.

I am so over myself, why aren't you?

It comes from self-serving judgments, comparing to one other, and it is another road to nowhere. I am so pissed off at the petty ego lurking inside all of the beautiful and endearing women/mothers. Why don't women treat other mothers like your own children, with loving kindness and no ego? It creates a path to love and the intent of our days is trying to make our wonderful children happy. The path of motherhood is so beautiful, but when it comes to self-love or respecting other adults' differences or unique opinions, the ego starts its dragon tirade and it causes great depths of unnecessary anxiety and discontent.

Our egos want us to discuss our self all day long and what the fuck we are going to do. Sigh. No one is that interesting or exciting! Believe me. The ego sucks all of the energy out of the room with our boring stories. It makes us say "me too" anytime a loved one or friend has gone to a faraway place or done something interesting or exciting. Why can't we just listen and allow others to speak and be heard? How does a fucking loud mouth like me, biggest one on the planet, learn this to be true? I see now what my father wanted from me. He urged me to take responsibility for my actions and be quiet so I could listen and be successful.

talking and not listening, sigh

Talking and not listening is ego. Talking and not listening is probably one of the most infuriating things I do to others, my poor family. I make excuses that it is ADD, but it really is impatience, which is a further ego problem. It is terrible! It is such a bad character flaw! How am I going to teach Brady anything if I am not listening to him? The new word for listening is mindful. It's disturbing for adults to learn how to listen. If friends are 100% talking they eventually lose me. I can't do it anymore. How can I be successful if I am unable to listen? How am I going to be a good friend if I don't listen?

the boredom of self-importance

Ladies and everyone, we are over our self-importance, it is no secret when someone is speaking we have to interrupt with your same story. They were trying to say something and our ego will not let them. The monologues of what happened to us good and bad have happened to the human being standing next to you. Did we forget to ask them about their lives 'cause you were talking about ours? We all have our own realities, which is very interesting and real. But just sometimes, and I hate when I catch myself doing this, I am discussing the idea behind this story, or Brady or I saw Nirvana at the Warfield in 1991 and I completely forgot to ask a colleague or friend how their life is going specifically. It makes me feel foolish. Sorry, I am calling it like I see it. Self-importance is very boring, mine is. Do all roads lead back to us? Still?

The most interesting idea I have discovered about others and myself is our expectation of what the universe delivered or did not deliver to us. In affluent America, women in particular want to be mothers (which is an honor like no other, to love others unconditionally is so cool) and have good health and warm shelter. When my life did not turn out the way I wanted it to, my story of look what happened to me was ongoing to the point of such boredom. I was boring myself how about everybody else I was talking to?

My ego gave me the right to shit talk, shout about what I deserved, talk so much about what I was going to do or not do, and I was like a rabid dog. I was as lost as the next human being on the planet, and I was so unhappy because no one would listen to me, and I wasn't getting what I deserved; respect, a job, a loving boyfriend, children, and a luxurious life. Look what happened to me: can you believe what others have done to me?

The more my ego thought of these things, the unhappier I became. My thoughts were creating my reality.

The instant I realized I should be 1) present and more giving in a relationship with a man, and not concentrating on what he should do for me 2) the moment I was going to do what I did not want to do (with my family and now during parenthood) and 3) begin to listen to others and stop projecting my bullshit stories, I was in instant relief.

best friends are our mirrors

In key friendships, with women, it is so important to cope, and be loving and caring (within reason) towards friends. I mean it is one thing to judge your family 'cause they are imperfect, it is normal to judge acquaintances, but it is important to love your friends and all of what they represent, because you picked them as an adult, right? If any friendships are not working for me on any level, I will lovingly let go. Best friends have to be honest with one another, and like in marriage we should be able to hear truths. They don't say it to me to be vindictive; they want me to be a better person and have some pure dignity. Right? That is how I see it.

I did not experience competitive behavior in women like I see now. What an ego game that everyone is losing. I was never in the game, 'cause I was working and globetrotting. I cannot understand the green eyes in women on everything, from children, to clothes, to what you do, what you don't do, to your marriage, how many mirrors you have in your beautiful house, its exhausting. I had no idea how petty adults were, not at all.

When I was growing with my friendships, I only felt encouragement and excitement for the continual adventure. Are you with me? Let's go!

We could do anything except compare ourselves and judge others all day long. What an ego trip. Do we like to feel less than others? Why not take care of others, run for office, and contribute to the universe to fulfill our destinies? The universe sure needs everybody right now! We could get a full time job of course, and that will promise to kick our ass! Or we can allow bitterness to take a hold on us and resent our very darling partners for doing everything we asked of them or lose one friend after too much gossip and judgment behind a closed door. We can stop discussing the negative events and people that bring us down, just a consideration. This is taking down the best humans at the moment. Why can't we cope with life when someone (especially) or something is not ideal? I am guilty of all of this shit.

Why has insincerity become a life's path? Do you suppose it creates unhappiness?

My ego will flare if someone does not accept a sincere apology or I believe loved ones could listen more, which says everything about me! I should remember how to detach from these events so I can be the productive and inspired person I write about being. What I mean by detaching is 1) not discussing what this person or event did to me 2) not talking about a person who I believe did me wrong or 3) not letting my head have bad thoughts at all.

holding on to feel bad

Why do we dislike another for the petty things that happened in the past? We can't let that go for the sake of surviving unhappiness in our lives? Our petty ego convinces us that this is acceptable behavior. We should listen to the way we attach to people and events that bring us down. We seem to love it somehow.

ego choices

When I was at the end of my rainbow, or rope, whatever you want to call it, I realized that my life and situation had everything to do with not listening to my intuition and reacting to rejection for the first time (boy did I make a journey out of that). All while drinking and falling down with my self-importance. In certain countries there are no choices who to marry or have children with. Our issues of negativity and complaining are futile when you look outside of your street, city or country.

comparing is ego too

People seem to love to compare themselves to anybody and everyone. If you are an <u>adult</u>, and believe that what you feel, say or do is better, your ego has misguided you once again. Adults are in such pain over this.

Adults spend lots of time talking what they do, how much better they do it, that I may die from listening to it. I am trying to get a grip on this and think to myself, is this all there is? Who is better than whom? How smart their kids are? How rich they are? What? It is adults going on and on about their own self-importance with no listening? I am in shock how small we are when it comes to our boasting or our limited emotional generosity.

I come from an ego family of limited encouragement and reactive behavior. I figured out through my friendships that loving others and listening without judgment could be a great journey.

the envy journey

Envy is laughing at us. It's a competition we are having with ourselves. Jane Kane, my mother, gave me great advice once. She said lose your jealousy and envy toward others because it will it will take you down hard. It's bad energy. She recommended, often, "don't even go there!" Once I became a mother, I could sense the ubiquity of envy, in all of us. Before Brady, I was getting a job, recovering from divorce, managing my attention deficit mishaps (for real), moving residences, etc. to ever notice this unfortunate way of behaving. Be careful of envy even if your family or circle of friends indulge in it. Envy is bad karma.

Envy is petty, self-involved, whining, copying without responsibility, whispering, miserable, deceitful, infantile, defeating, and insincere. I had no idea how lost and envious we are, on every level that exists. There can never be enough praise, adoration, or complimenting, for any of us. The ego is insatiable let's be honest!

Social media reveals ego, sincerity and insincerity at its best. It's a truth seeker because there are friends that reciprocate sincerely online and others that refuse! Social media is very indicative. How many times did I have an ego meltdown writing the sincerity story and for how many years? Why do best friends creep other best friends? It's a sincere relationship right? I thought so. Social media outed you! This key envy gesture is attaching to what others have, don't have, and the continuation of comparing. I see us ego-tripping on envy, with best friendships & mothers & coaches & adults & parents (its meant for children, teenagers & young adults, right?). Oh my god, it is entertainment and tragedy at its best. Adults are competitive because someone walked through the front door. This is the best we can do after being given so much? Well look at the US government currently, a bunch of infants serving their self-importance sentence 101.

Even better, when you ask the universe for what someone has or is (and when you attain it, because you asked for it) now everyone is envious of "you". It is a circle of self-defeat. I thought envy (competitive nature with everything) only existed in Ivy League universities, corporate culture, competitive sports, entertainment industries, with Wall Street moguls! They're the ego players right?

We are distracted by seeking praise. We have created uber bullying on social media by teaching our young adults to seek and demand approval. We have put our wildlife & mother earth in harms way from our addiction to oil, plastic, meat, etc. It is self-involved behavior that creates unhappiness. Cheers you won!

I let go of what I am supposed to have, with whom, where and how a very long time ago. If I am <u>not comparing</u> everything and everyone to my ideas, thoughts, conversations, life experiences, religion, finances, lifestyle, thought process, worldly travels, and anything else I am missing? If I am living in sincerity and removing envy whenever possible, I can give genuine compliments. I am happy for others success. I understand others shortcomings, who am I to judge? I am sincere, yahoo my favorite. I learn from my differences with others. I am truthful, which is not easy in the ego world today.

I am humbled which is a practice by now. I am not feeling less because I don't have enough or feel better because I have more. I am not taking score because we are not in a fucking competition. Luckily, when I accepted that others success, happiness, were none of my concern, it was a relief!

Careful of your green thoughts today! Are you?

If I am proud of my thoughts about others and situations, etc. and I am focused on others good behavior towards others and me, then I am in a state of mindful contribution to others on any level. If I am focused on getting along with Toddy when he is wrong (wink wink), and I am refraining from comparing myself to others, which is a bunch of shit, while letting go of my self importance, then nothing can go that wrong, right?

Chapter 7

the zen in me

On my 42nd a birthday when tears appeared because my pregnancy test was negative, Todd brought home a grey-colored puffa bunny, tiny and dear. It was a Netherlands dwarf bunny that drew my love charge like a sparkler on the 4th of July. I could not stop talking, petting, writing, discussing, kissing or looking at this heavenly creature who I allowed to bumble all over my house. I was on the ground petting that little rabbit for hours on end, running up and down the stairs for organic lettuce, taking him to the vet and announcing my love for him. My bunny exemplified my love because I couldn't receive anything from him but a ruffle and a thump. Most people understand this, but my ego heart learned much later. The bunny would dreamy-eye belly and me roll in his nest of infant blankets under my bed. My bunny brought out the Zen in me. One of the life coach's on 2007 Twitter tweeted there is "no awakening like a human's love for an animal." I didn't have a baby, but I loved a bunny. I used to write poetry about my bunny and my family and friends were so kind about it (sigh). Poor Toddy so wanted me to "rub" him like I did the bun bun! Puff was the first baby I ever had. Lucky me.

Brady the bumbling Viking

To care and love and nurture a bunny is a simpler task than loving a big bumbling baby of a human. Oh boys, they are crazy and cute at the same time! My baby man is taking me down with the biggest smile on his face every step of the day. You know that to conceive a baby at my age of 44 was epic for an amateur like me, but it did not matter because I had my yummy stud of a muffin Toddy to help! Nothing will prepare you for a child. No one tells the truth! Oh, and when they do, you are, like, that mom, what a bitch. Then you have a baby and you are, like, moms were not complaining (bitching) enough! It is unbelievable.

Brady arrived on Jan 7th 2008 on a sunny brisk day in Mineola, NY! His arrival came during Jerry Garcia's most poetic song (which is a stroke of luck) and he has been loved happily ever after. He had bow lips, light red hair, could cry so loudly and is just one of the cutest guys out there. We have been giggling ever since. Every child is an amazing bright light! And they will challenge you and kick your fat fucking ass till the cows come home and you better like every moment of it. Ha ha, Mommy, you are going down. Don't make everything I do and say about you either, Mommy! The cool part of parenthood is and Mr. Campbell said, when you transcend from one self is when the colorful and enriching experience begins. It does and it is!

So if the spiritual healers are correct, then maybe, 1) the laws of attraction can be helpful for drawing beings and events in your life 2) once you get your heart and home in order 3) then mindfulness can create a happy and bright reality?

I am grateful that my dream of having a family took place later. I am trying to learn how to breathe, to be in a constant state of giving (from a place of strength) and be thoughtful with every moment. As I grow, I am focusing on the positivity that the earth has to offer, which it does.

happy thoughts, happy life

The laws of attraction can be helpful when manifesting a sexy relationship, a family, career or goodwill, right? It's not a proven science but trying to be in a positive light is fun anyway! With this idea in mind, we can have hope for ourselves, and our global family.

Mother Theresa mentioned, that, if you can, be in a positive light every day, which is love and be kind even if others are unkind, the game can change for the better. That is a game changer, really. All we have to do right in this world is love everybody and everything for what they are. Once you realize that thought patterns and thoughtful discussions in our mind should be noticed at all times, you are on the way. When I was in deep struggles with my ego (that bad girl), I kept saying why am I such a bad student, why does my boss dislike me, why can't I get that job? Why don't they include me? Why didn't they say I'm doing a good job? Perhaps I was having an internal dialogue to myself that was creating these circumstances.

> *"I was in relief because of self-acceptance and more so, acceptance of others."*
> —kkshaw47

During this time, of letting go, as we say, thank you Buddha! I was in relief because of self-acceptance and more so, acceptance of others. It was working in a positive way to create my short & long-term reality. I thought, I get to participate in loving the universe back!

Is manifesting real?

Once I chose acceptance I felt much more in control. Once I got over myself (lost my self importance) I felt happier. I was willing to work, to fail at anything and keep working even if the result was not what I wanted. I could feel my thoughts moving from my "self", even though I was not a parent yet. Could the Laws of Attraction manifest a beautiful, bouncy boy for me? Could it create the marriage I imagined? Could my thoughts build a happy household, maybe a little less bubbly than the home I grew up in, which was awesome because it was mine?

The ideas behind the Laws of Attraction are exciting because it is a visual pattern that can create a physical reality. I call that the possibility of magic. It's so exciting! How about I am continually trying to monitor my thoughts, by keeping the sun in and the dark out? Yahoo!

I feel tipsy because my idea of love came true. I have to say that I was very fortunate with loving boyfriends when I was younger. I do not know how that was, but these boys were badass, gentle and kind! After getting stepped on a little bit, I wanted to find a partner who would like to strive for an inspiring and healthy life together. Who would think this would happen after being rejected? Thank you for dumping me husband #1 so I could get to this "place." My head is still swirling that I live in NY of all places. Where are the flowers please?

My head is spinning because I am a mommy of a fourth grader at 54 years old. Oh my dear goodness, being a parent is like nothing else. You better eat your Wheaties, take your vitamins (organic) and buckle that seat belt 'cause you are going to need it. I am shaking my head and smiling because Brady kicks my ass all day long. I love it and I deserve it. I am tipsy that I have a place I can call home; I am drunk from love and with my dish of a husband. The Secretini is better (that is manifesting good thoughts to create a happy reality), than any dirty martini. Cheers lambs!

Power of now

The ego seems to have an important role in our relationships. It helps us grow and conquer but it can have devastating results when conflict arises in our full-grown adult lives.

Tolle says, "A genuine relationship is one that is not dominated by the ego with its image-making and self-seeking. In a genuine relationship, there is an outward flow of open, alert attention toward the other person in which there is no wanting whatsoever."

He asks, "Is there a difference between happiness and inner peace? Yes. Happiness depends on conditions being perceived as positive; inner peace does not."

And he adds, "Being spiritual has nothing to do with what you believe and everything to do with your state of consciousness."

It was clear how, if I remove my "attachment of self" from everything (especially unfavorable conflicts), then life could be very peaceful and simple.

Once I moved to LI and started to put the house together and had a baby, which will bring out your true self, I asked myself how could I lose self importance in the community (I had been gone for a long time)? How could I be a nurturing partner (without making everything about me) and have the strength to be a parent at my age, while managing the marriage? As I mentioned before, it was Cindy's suggestion to watch Oprah Winfrey's New Earth and interpretation of Eckhart Tolle. What she explained very succinctly is that if we remove our ego from everything we could have a more humane and peaceful planet. While observing others I was relieved to learn that if I detach from my egoistical thoughts and destructive behavior from all unfavorable situations, then I am off the hook! I can let go of thinking what I deserve (expectations) or being right. I can be a better partner in marriage this time. I can be aware of being a domineering parent. Thankfully. I can give love and light.

I got over myself when I was given a gift to love my yummy husband and my dear son. I was, like, I am going to do whatever I am supposed to do and not complain, which is a tall order for my child of an ego.

My father Tom was the king of L&M cigarettes, black coffee and Pinot Grigio until the end. After his long career in defense, he retired very successfully and nested in Babylon with my mother in 1991 and became a significant contributor to the community, with his duty and time. He was an active member of The Rotary Club and on the board of the building zones in Babylon. He was a respected guy for his high flying salesmanship and his quiet humble demeanor later on. He read every line of every page of the NY Times ever since I could remember.

jane and tom awakening

Coming home to my parents in 2003 was the best present I ever gave myself. Yahoo thank you to my intuition. The first week home I thought I would hate myself for returning home to live with them. I remember, true Tom and Jane fashion, they were like, fuck you, we don't need your negativity. Their reactive crazy is 100% each and every time. If I threw mud they slung it right back at me. Their ironclad response to my self-loathing was a good kick in the face. It turned me around immediately. Each day, I had a plan for what I could do for them instead of running out of the door with my friends to laugh and drink coffee somewhere, you know? So each day I was going to the doctors, grocery store, dry cleaners, and local dinner spots. It was an awakening. I felt content and home life was wonderful.

As I mentioned early on, I was staying in my old room, with

my work clothes. I woke up so early each morning to catch the 7am train to Manhattan. I am thinking how did I get here? How did I go from the gorgeous Bay Area to this shit hole of NY again? I found myself walking while the moon was up in my new Anne Taylor sales rep clothes, getting a cup of coffee to run up the stairs to the train, and breaking a sweat just while the doors are closing. It was NY at its best. Then I took the #2 train down to Tribeca to Chamber Street to this old and dusty office.

On the way home I walked, trying not to disturb Tom and Jane during pre dinner hour. My mother made dinner for my father every night that she could. They would be so cheerful and happy to see me walk through the door. My father was the cutest guy especially after 1-2 drinks. His wit was at its best and he was a fun silly buzzed. This was in between seven cigarette breaks before dinner. The dude mainlined cigarettes ever since I can remember. My father and I became especially close during the early morning hours. My father, brother, and I are early risers, which was a special pact with us. The best thing was simply to sit in the kitchen together not talking, him reading the NY Times in full, and me sitting they're looking at photos in a fashion or tabloid magazine. I would ask him any question that popped into my head on sports or politics. He would give me a razor sharp answer, never wavering, like Toddy.

I was home for almost one year. My mother during this time was out of her mind on the progress of the romance of Mr. Todd Shaw. My father and I were entertained and sometimes annoyed by her insistence on knowing what was going on.

As I mentioned earlier, we were married on Nov 20th of that year. I was so happy because Tom was there and he could be really proud of me for marrying such a gentle, smart, decent man like Todd. Tom and I danced under the wedding star lights of the Manhattan loft that evening to JT's "How sweet it is to be loved by you."

We all get ditsy in our older years. I feel it now. But my mother had noticed that my dad was becoming vague. He had to be lifted up from the table at our wedding and into the limo and up to the Benjamin Hotel, and not from too many Pinot Grigios like usual. His body was beginning to shut down and his wires were not connecting.

We always had a mellow attitude towards my father's health; even though he did everything he could to destroy himself, mostly with cigarettes. His partying had subsided during the years that we are supposed to do, right?

The days spent with my parents and fourteen years ago being married to Todd was probably the best times of my life. We soon moved out to Amityville, which was so much closer than San Francisco! And they came to see us so often for coffee, tea and Sunday dinners. And we always had drinks and laughs and I am grateful for that time. Once Brady was born it was even better. My father made such an effort to play and be with Brady. At Brady's first birthday party, I recall my neighbor Lauren saying to me, "Your dad did not say one word today." And she was saying it because she was concerned. He was a quiet man, sick of hearing himself speak just like me, so it was not that unusual. Something was off though.

We were noticing him slip away a little bit. In fact each morning, my mother and I would speak and say – is he alive today? Go in his bedroom and see if he is still breathing and he always was, for years. He would bumble down the stairs and get cracking on those L&M cigarettes.

Each Sunday dinner he ate less and became quieter, but we did not know what it could be. He had been going to his everyday doctor and blood was being taken, and so everything seemed normal.

I had planned a parents' dinner for the first day of spring for my parents and my sister in law's parents and our old time friends. That morning I got a call from my mother Friday March 20 and she said, "Kristen, I am taking Tom to ER at Southside in Bay Shore. His blood pressure is furiously high, so meet me there."

We were somehow relieved that he was going to a hospital so we could figure out what was really happening. When I met them in the ER that day, he was himself. I walked in with a venti latte, and while he was hooked up to multiple IVs, he ripped the coffee out of my hand and drank the entire thing. He was a fierce caffeine junkie like my sister and I. That's our Tom! We spent several hours with him in the ER and then we had to leave.

That was the last time I ever saw him as the person I knew. From the ER he went right up to ICU. Not only was there a tumor wrapped around his pulmonary artery, he had completely flipped out from withdrawal from cigarettes. He had not one cigarette after that and I am certain that was a detox like no other. The poor guy, being sick, could not articulate how sick and terrible he was feeling from lack of carcinogens. The next day we went to the ICU and he was on a ventilator and he was a shell of himself. His soul was preparing for the remarkable journey to heaven. He was still breathing, but Tom, (my father) was not there.

His entire family came and after several weeks, he rallied and perked up a little bit but ended up on the terminally ill floor. We would bring him milk shakes and cheer him up, but his flight had begun. The cold spring months were dismal and during that time they certainly were. I remember one day I went to visit him during his three-week stay and he slept the whole time and I just sat there admiring him and watching over him for several hours. He knew that I was there. He had a catheter in his lungs and the day they took it out we knew it was time to let him go. He moved from Southside hospital to an amazing hospice facility on Arnold Avenue in West Babylon. Jane, my mother, her best friend Irene Morris (who just lost her husband Bob three months before) were there as they transported Tom from the gurney to his hospice bed. His brown eyes looked blue deep blue to me like his mother's eyes, and he was barely hanging on.

I took his hand in mine and said, "Dad, its me, KK. Can you hear me? I am right here. Please hold my hand. I want you to know we are always going to be together no matter what happens. I am part of you and you me and we will always be together. Please don't forget this." I can thank my dear friend Jenny Cahill Ford for telling me this once, and giving me this very important message from above. It was so helpful for me during this time. Love you Jenny!

And he replied I know, but he felt so terrible that he could not really focus. I wanted to go back to visit him at hospice, but I was anxious because Brady was 18 months old and my father could be difficult because he always wanted to get up and leave which was hard to convince him to stay.

I was so troubled when I came home from hospice that day, I remember telling my best friend Laurie who was babysitting "This is it, he is leaving soon." I was choking that day on my own breath. I could not get out of my own way and I was so exhausted from the draining experience of preparing to lose a family member. My poor mother. Finney my puppy of curls, kept me going outside in the cold sunshine with Brady in his carriage.

With tears streaming down my face right now, I can only be moved by the love and care that goes on when a family member leaves you. I was not well that day and I know why, because he was leaving us.

The loving part of the family is what breaks (opens) my heart when someone passes away. Our family had so many wonderful times together, so much laughter. When my brother and sister and I were adults my parents were so much more present and interested in spending time with us. There was never a day or night that my mother and father did not welcome us into their home. We had so many wonderful dinners together and laughter till the sun set.

good grief!

Following his passing, a book, written by a hospice nurse was put into my mailbox from a neighbor. She knew the feelings that I had since her father had passed away recently. It was the story of passing and heaven and light and what a relief it is for those entering. I was profoundly sad when I thought of my attachment to his passing. When I thought about how difficult it would be for him to reside here and that he could be "safe" in heaven, I was in emotional control.

I was and am in complete acceptance of my father's passing and so happy for him that he fulfilled his destiny. I am hopeful that he learned about himself and the power of profound love on his journey to heaven. When I considered my father's feelings of relief by letting go, and letting go of my feelings and only thinking of his, it was so simple.

Chapter 8

with all this bliss today, no ego, thank you!

Being married is awesome. I, however, have to get over myself to be happy. After a couple of cycles of relationships with men, I see a common thread. Men are all darling. Men are all noble. Men are smart and listen to the best music! However, at times, men are profoundly self unaware of their inadequacies. Sorry lambs its what I see! Women have been putting our inadequacies on the cover magazines since the beginning of time. See the difference here? Todd is so gracious when I bash men for their violence or deceptions. In general, men are in great need of self-reflection and responsibility with conflict resolution of themselves in relationships. I do not know if Tony Robbins, the great life coach can save <u>all</u> of you. You also need to get over your self-absorbed or overly spirited jolly asses! Do men get so buzzed so frequently because they have nothing better to do? Men are so hard working and they do not get time on their own to think things through 'cause they are out in the wilderness of their careers. Self-awareness would be a very good tool for men today, and we love how you guys provide for us, we do!

However, men are continually comparing themselves to everyone and if they fall short, their egos get bruised and you better watch out for the <u>wrath</u>. Right you guys?

In many petty conflicts, men, demonstrate reactive behavior. If we look at the global playing field and the lack of leadership in responsibility on many levels, it could be a truth! Here at the Shaws' we are trying to work through our conflicts. 1% we are good and the rest not very. I honestly, and God is my witness, try and eat the dirt being handed to me and not react when Todd and I are having it out! It's an ego pull like no other.

living for each other - Buddha

Aside from our seldom ego pulling, we are in a positive relationship. Both Todd and I came to this marriage with a lot of good and not good times. Experience taught us to get over ourselves and to focus on the importance of moving our union forward. This has been a positive element to our relationship so far. In our household we are living for each other. We are both somewhat submissive (Todd is going to hate this). It is a Buddhist non-ego message that if we are <u>living for each other</u> nothing can go that wrong because no one has a hall pass, to be selfish except for Brady, which he is. We are not thinking of what the universe owes us 'cause we are working towards the other's happiness, and are humbled by our love for one another, today. I hope tomorrow too!

over serving me, myself

One evening early in our marriage, I had a big girls night at the house in Amityville. I am in jeans and clunky high heels ready for my girls' nite to begin. I am sipping my Sonoma California grape like a fountain and in mid-glass, Todd looks at me with genuine seriousness and goes, "Kristen please be careful of those big fat red ruby grapes tonight." It was girls night right?

Silence. Pause. Silence. Typically, my infant ego would defend my intentions that evening so I could do exactly what I wanted? Right? Isn't that how it goes?

I looked at him and my intuition mouthed the words, "You are right. I am not doing my high volume, meaningless bullshit, don't you think I'm sexy black out ways tonight." And it has a bonus, I was not sick the day after.

It was a turning point again, that my truth was harsh, but necessary. It was necessary roughness, right? I was so glad that someone I love could tell me what is right. Toddy, thank you for calling me out on my weakness, because you love me.

Shortly following that gourmet pizza and wine blitz, I was organizing a dinner out with my girl friends in Babylon. Yahoo! Combing my hair, putting earrings on, getting my purse all ready for a nice night out dinner and delicious mixology. Just as I left the house with the keys in my hand, Todd looks up and says, "Hon. do not sip at all tonight, please."

Silence. Pause. Silence. Girls night out.

I said to him, "You got it babe. No worry."

My husband cocktails like everybody else. Leaving that night, I could have said, "Why what are you talking about? This is my night out with the girls, etc. I never get to get out on my own why can't I have one with dinner?" And I knew this message had more meaning, if I am the one passing around the "we have to do what is asked of others", then I have to do it, first.

writing is not your priority

Being married for the last fourteen years and a mom is so fun because I started a family, late in life. It is the new normal and a new life for me. If I were talking about cleaning the house 15 years ago it would not sound like me. So now, the moment

I think I can leave my house disorganized, I am wrong. One evening I came home, to a cluttered house in every corner you could see. I came home that very night to a frowning Todd. 'KK, the house is a mess and he was disapproving." And my reactive crazy starts saying, what are you kidding me? Everyone says that our house is so sunshine colors and designed! Get over it and you never give me compliments about anything, by the way. Fuck you dude." I stamped upstairs like a child. When I came back down, thinking I was right, which is a Virgo 100% of the time, I was wrong. Todd was not giving me an apologetic glance. He was disappointed in the fact that the house is all a clutter! He said, "KK, I pay the bills, I do laundry, I cook, I do what you ask of me, I take Brady away for hours so you can blog, twitter and write about what you want, but first, and I am just asking here, is that you keep the house neat and tidy please, after Brady, because that is your priority, not writing!"

Fade to grey.

Todd was right.

I had to listen to what he was asking of me within reason and deliver. Done. I am on it. I try to keep the house uncluttered so we do not have anger flare ups. The super fucked up messy drawers tug on our egos often, but we keep trying to get it right. Todd will be so glad I admitted this right now.

being present for brady

I am astounded by how my distractions, actions and what I say, can make or break a situation with Brady.

Parenthood has been especially good for a super space cadet like me. Being the youngest is easy, you fly under the radar and you do not have to implement and do things. I am very good at talking and writing, but <u>doing</u> for me is a challenge. My family and friends will tell you that I am exhausting. Brady's darling smart self is testing me physically, curiously every moment of every day. I am not used to someone needing me, much less asking me questions. I used to require a lot of attention as a child. Hugging, talking, pushing, asking, wanting, yelling, falling, crying, and singing all day long. That is a job of a dear child. When Brady was younger, he would get into trouble because I was distracted by his need for attention.

Being a parent requires taking responsibility for your thoughts and actions. It takes it to a whole higher level. I am astounded how <u>my</u> actions and what I say can make or break a situation with my son. And just about every time he gets in trouble for something - it is because of what I said or did (unintentionally of course) to create this final result.

My impatience is epically indulgent when we are in a conflict. Impatience is my worst offender. My lack of focus is wrong on my part. I do not care if I have ADD, it is imperative that each day I find a way to Brady, through listening or playing or sharing. Being interactive with a young child is getting easier for me. I had no idea what real presence was! I always pray for presence with Brady. Help me listen better and not be distracted. Being present is a desire I have as a parent.

It is easy for me to love others when all is going my way. If I turn around and say "oh Brady, I love you baby." and he looks at me with dead silence and out the window, I am like oh, get over yourself, mommy.

managing ego in reactive behavior, sigh

The key concept of not reacting is huge with adults. Being a nice and loving person comes more easily to some people than others. It's just the way it is, right? So once we have our life in its place (of our perception), how do we keep our ego out of petty conflicts? The ego ignites petty conflicts in the first place. We are not fooling anyone, here, you or me!

If you have a conflict with a friend or someone was offensive towards you, which is part of life, right adults? What do you typically do? Take them down? Talk non-stop about it and/or you repeat the story, look what happened and can you believe it? Or better, you mirror their behavior and make it worse?

I am surprised that as adults, we are incapable of walking away from petty conflict and never ever letting it go." Bad behavior from others is part of life and reactive crazy, makes it worse. Why haven't we learned that betrayal or bad behavior towards us is 100% part of life and that we should have the emotional intelligence to be free from it? We all lose our minds when some mud is thrown in our face. We all have a story like this! Why is there reactive crazy meltdown town when a loved one shares a single, unfavorable truth with us? If I have honest relationships, then aren't I going to be better? Being honest seems to be a hard thing to do in adulthood. It makes my relationships less trustworthy, less rich in flavor. When I allow my loved ones to share a truth, I just have to listen. I find honesty refreshing and hilarious. The truth is illuminating to me.

Give me some of that honesty and I am good to go – can I give you a sample too? Our ego is cloaking our truths all day long and we are such infants because of it. Let the infants be infants already!

I love my family for their honesty and letting go when a conflict does arise. My mother especially is a person that you can get in a drag out fight with horns on fire, and she will never agree with you while in a conflict, ever. However, if you say you are sorry in a sincere way, she will let it go – right out the window. I learned recently that I was not as good at letting things go as my mother, from Todd. Todd is all about living in the present and letting go of what has happened in the past, for the most part. I am so happy that I grew up this way. When I start to feel crazy about others actions or my own silly self-importance, --I let it go and it feels great. Cheers!

accepting apologies without forgiveness, wtf?

Our egos interfere with apologies all day long. Many times I have been a horrendous asshole with my ego being brutally honest at the wrong time, going to tell someone else how to feel because of my experiences, (I don't think so), or did not say something when maybe I should have, and when I have delivered an apology I meant it. Why do we expect apologies when we can't even accept them?

Forgiveness can be a very positive tool to work with. That means accepting an apology when it is delivered especially from someone we love, whom has given us love, adoration, and compliments throughout the relationship.

Who likes to be in the state of insincerity? Do you? I'm just asking. Are we waiting around for someone to wrong us so that we can resent him or her? What does that say about us? And when someone has hurt my feelings, I accept their apology so that I can move on? How many of us will not accept an apology? Why do people say they have accepted the apology, but they haven't? Do they then have control over you? It is their pass to resent you and they get to live in a state of passive aggressiveness (that they could very well deny, which is crazier) or insincerity? Let's please stop this ego roller coaster ride.

this bliss

With all this bliss, I am not about to let my ego take it away. It ain't happening. If I apply the law of non-stop loving and giving that I am learning in parenthood, to my key relationships, then nothing can go that wrong right?

If I am in a continual state of kindness (which is love right?) with others, if I am unattached to others' unfavorable actions, and I am getting over my judgments of others (which is self serving,) then we're all good, right?

If I am a partner doing whatever my husband asks of me, if I am losing my self importance and what the universe owes me, if I manage my reactive and defending behavior then there is a chance for an emotionally successful life, right?

I should not have one bad day if the universe "delivered" for me. I am not going to let my ego tug at the calm that exists in my marriage today (and tomorrow too), I am not going to let my ego disrupt my presence while being a mother and I am taking responsibility for everything I am feeling (good/bad), in every relationship. Thank you Buddha, Mr. Chopra, Mr. Campbell, His Holiness, Mr. Eckhart Tolle and our beautiful Mother Theresa and all the sincerity the world has to offer!

There, I said it, now let's have a sip of sincerity with a splash of lemon sunshine!

Chapter 9

sincerity is good karma

I thrive on honesty, I mean I think I do, right? I have to beat down my ego, now since I wrote the no ego book! I better be careful of myself!

We need sincerity to attract positive energy and true love. The most valuable gift I possess is sincerity. It has served me in my polar ego swings, lack of focus from ADD and reactive behavior when I am defensive. I would be anxious if I have had dark conversations in my mind while speaking to others in a light tone. It is not normal, sorry. Insincerity is the worst ego moves. I never questioned this until recently. Some of us live in passive aggressive behavior because the truth is too much to bear? This is where the sincerity begins to break down and lose its power. This means we don't speak the truth, even to love ones from a place of sincerity, because the reactive meltdown is too much to bear and honestly it goes on for lifetimes. I thrive on honesty, I mean I think I do, right? I always have to be beating down my ego, especially now since I wrote this book regarding no ego behavior too! I better be careful of myself!

get over it please and fire that ego today – kkshaw47

Sincerity is part of trustworthy relationships and there is little of "it" out there because of our egos right there like the manic devil trying to take us down. If I am insincere with my key relationships, there is no point to anything, ever. As an adult I am shocked how insincere we are as individuals. We are unable to hear the truth regarding our character defects. How about we try and adjust it and a way to look at our selves clearly?

Or we can't let go of some bullshit that happened so many years ago and we're holding on to it--after the apology? WTF, really? The point is that I could understand ego, insincerity and other character defects which get in the way of our path to love, in the workplace, like all of my sales pits, with the shit talking of others and insincerity going on right and left, but not in our children's schools and in our communities, right? So this is the license to be insincere and we like it like that? I do not know if the laws of the universe think this is a good idea, at all.

Perhaps our insincerity came from a place where a loved one hurt our feelings terribly, and we were too cowardly to tell them so, thinking that they would not listen or love us any longer.

Sincere people are joyful to be with. I think I learned it from my girlfriends. I do not say things that I don't mean or mean what I don't say. What the fuck is that about? Where does insincerity come from? Is it self-importance fueling our jealousy, our comparing, judging, and our reactive bullshit? We are not fooling anyone, by the way. Our insincerity is glaringly apparent. It is making us look like self-serving assholes and I am not certain it becomes us, ever.

My mother Jane Kane is a great strong gal who displays many presentations of self-importance, but she is a sincere person. That's why everyone loves her so much.

Many times we are all looking to lash out of what others have done to us that are "unfavorable". We forget all the love and compliments they have given us throughout the years. We are accepting apologies with insincerity because we have nothing better to do with our time, because we have it all, right? I mean, come on, people, get over it and fire that ego, today. It does not support goodwill, at all.

be careful of self importance

Is it self-involved behavior again? The continual state of self possession, where others have to think, act, have the same family unit, same friends, our children have to have the friends we want, the same god we worship, speak the same language as us, and lastly, have the same sex we do. Negativity begins and becomes a raging force. We provoke others to see our perspective, even if it calls for untruths. Sigh.

Insincerity (self importance) causes mothers, fathers, mothers, fathers, coaches, colleagues, soldiers, politicians, teachers, healthcare workers, friends, to be resentful (cause you have nothing better to do) of others and unhappy. I question the depths of sincerity of everybody. What is the point of <u>anything</u> if we are not sincere? Because if I am sincere then, I am truthful which is what we teach the kids all day long right? I am sorry for a mistake I made, my goodness we are only humans, not perfect. I listened to a truth I needed to hear in order to grow. I love you, which is what we seem to be continually looking for. I am forgiving of mistakes others have made because they are human and I have to get over it. I meant what I said because I am sincere (but you know that already). I apologize for the misunderstandings because that is what it is. Thank you because sincerity gives me manners and thank god, my thoughts mirror my actions. I was wrong (without yelling) and lastly, you were right! What is the point of sincerity if we let self-importance take us down all day long? Self-importance is an ego behavior lurking under the surface of our insincerity. I began my life as an outspoken demanding and domineering kid, but I was always sincere. It seems self importance is destroying us on a level not to be believed. The obstacle to the path of happiness – is self-involvement, self-importance, and ego – choose your flavor of poison. Everyone and everything is self-centered and there is no end in sight! It has destroyed families, broken the best of friendships (this is the best we can do?), it is the cause of divorce and ultimately put the world in harm's way of our own inner superior beliefs. I am not a psychologist and I can figure this out. Nothing can go wrong if our good thoughts and actions are in harmony.

If we can lose our self-importance (ego) with everybody & everything, we _may_ get some relief from, ourselves. I let go of a petty conflict, immediately (especially with Todd) I accept an apology with forgiveness in a sincere manner. I am free of shit talking (oh that again), I am observing my own actions (not attaching to unproductive people/events) I am truthful with my loved ones in a thoughtful way. I am listening without interrupting (oh god!) and owning my mistakes. I am _not_ looking for what my loved ones have "not done" for me and lastly, I am not comparing my actions to others' actions. This is relief at long last! So, if my heart is in charge, and I am losing all negativity while living in a state of loving forgiveness, that way I am "for real", right?

more envy

Envy is relentless. Until I became a mother, I had no idea of the ubiquity of envy, in all of us. From what I can see, and I could be wrong, it comes from lack of childhood and/or self-experience. I thought envy existed in corporate America and politics! I had no idea how lost and envious we are. Why don't we teach the children about the pitfalls of envy and its ugly raging heaving burden of resentment in grade school? My mother, Jane Kane's, best advice of my entire life was, "don't be envious, or jealous. It shows how weak and off-center you are." I took that advice to heart and it served me well. The problem is many of us are fucking ego-tripping hardcore on envy. Oh my god, it is entertainment and tragedy at its best.

petty competitive

I let go of what I am supposed to have, with whom, where and how a long time ago. If I do not compare everything and everyone to my ideas, thoughts, conversations, life experiences, religion, finance, lifestyle, thought process, worldly travels, children's livelihoods and anything else I am missing? I'm good to go! I love people unconditionally, I am happy for their success, I understand their short comings, I am sincere, I learn from our differences, I am truthful, I am honest, I am not feeling less 'cause I do not have enough, I am not feeling more 'cause I have so much, and I am not taking score and we are not in a fucking competition. Petty competitive comes from insincerity that is another self-deceiving and self-important ego move.

A pure heart or sincerity, will take out the weak, defensive ego, every time. It is a productive life strategy.

Conclusion

When I reflect, my ego has been very useful for me growing up as a child and a young adult. The ego is responsible for 1) starting many inventions 2) heroes' stories 3) sports championships 4) love & 5) friendships. It helped me start and finish this story. It is a driving force within us, it's just that as we grow and humble we should learn how to let go of its grasp so tightly, in order to be happy.

And now being humbled in life and becoming a parent, picking a super cheerful, colorful bouquet of friends back here in Babylon village, while losing my self importance and judgment to travel through life's abyss, by checking my reactive behavior in marriage totally (working on it lol), while listening and being present for Brady Bug, while observing the heartfelt, wild, scary, beautiful, distant, loving, adoring, terrorizing, heartbreaking, twisted, happy, devastating, adventurous future ahead for Todd, Brady and myself, that other people's realities, stories and ways to happiness are more interesting than mine. Sincerity could have attracted positive energy into my day to day and perhaps love too!

Share with me, if you would please, a large glass of this sincerity w a splash of happy. Let's blend our thoughts, words and actions into a glass of healthy detachment, self control and sunshine, it's a relief, I promise.

Chapter 10

Living in bliss, letting go, creating karma guide

Friends

If four riends' happiness is more important than our own, we are good to go

Do not talk shit of others because it is a reflection of our negativity.

Stop comparing to make ourselves to look better; we cannot win 100% of the time.

Are our actions glaring or glowing at others?

Let our loved ones say truthful (unfavorable) things to us without our reactive crazy. Our friends love us so why can't we hear a truth, once?

Accept apologies 100% and move on. Right? Do we?

Stop attaching to friends actions as a sport – are we bored? This is an offender out there like no other, I see it in everyone and it comes from judging, which is self-serving.

Lose the continual judging. It is self serving.

Make sincerity a priority today.

Marriage

Men please work on self-awareness.

Women please let's work on strengthening ourselves by working toward independence. Stop telling our partners what we deserve, lol.

Do what our partner asks with a smile.

Lose resentment towards our husbands, we chose them.

Lose resentment towards our wive, we chose them.

Let go of self-importance to avoid divorce.

Accept apologies with sincerity.

Look at what our partners do for us (while avoiding the downside of denial)

Stop comparing ourselves to everybody.

Let our loved ones say truths without our reactive crazy behavior.

Stop attaching ourselves to you partners' actions all day long. Is that co-dependency?

Lose the judging due to lack of life experience.

Consider an unfavorable truth from our partner and take (3) steps to adjust it. It will build trust.

Make sincerity a priority today

Parenting

Men, please help mommy so she is not over worked.

Women, please write down what you need from your husband.

Do what our partner asks of us with a smile.

Let go of self-importance, it creates unhappiness.

Let's not compare our kids to everybody else, please.

Stop making everything our children do about us! Oh god.

Stop judging other parents; it is a reflection on us.

Be aware of our happy, present, detached, insecure, controlling, over bearing, domineering, and manipulative, and depressed characteristics.

Lose our own ego in our children's relationships – period. That's bullshit.

Accept apologies and move on. Do not make a conflict about <u>us</u> all day – don't we have better things to do?

Make sincerity a priority today.

58195834R00088

Made in the USA
Columbia, SC
17 May 2019